Discussing Child Abuse

Editor: Tracy Biram

Volume 388

independence
educational publishers

First published by Independence Educational Publishers

The Studio, High Green

Great Shelford

Cambridge CB22 5EG

England

© Independence 2021

Copyright

Photocopy licence

ISBN-13: 978 1 86168 846 0

Printed in Great Britain

Zenith Print Group

Contents

Introduction

Discussing Child Abuse is Volume 388 in the **issues** series. The aim of the series is to offer current, diverse information about important issues in our world, from a UK perspective.

ABOUT DISCUSSING CHILD ABUSE

In the UK one in five people are abused in one way or another in their childhood. This book looks at the different types of abuse, such as neglect and sexual, emotional and physical abuse and the long-lasting effects they have on the victims. But just how can children be protected? We explore ways in which safeguarding can help to spot signs of abuse and how it can be prevented.

OUR SOURCES

Titles in the **issues** series are designed to function as educational resource books, providing a balanced overview of a specific subject.

The information in our books is comprised of facts, articles and opinions from many different sources, including:

♦ Newspaper reports and opinion pieces

♦ Website factsheets

♦ Magazine and journal articles

♦ Statistics and surveys

♦ Government reports

♦ Literature from special interest groups.

A NOTE ON CRITICAL EVALUATION

Because the information reprinted here is from a number of different sources, readers should bear in mind the origin of the text and whether the source is likely to have a particular bias when presenting information (or when conducting their research). It is hoped that, as you read about the many aspects of the issues explored in this book, you will critically evaluate the information presented.

It is important that you decide whether you are being presented with facts or opinions. Does the writer give a biased or unbiased report? If an opinion is being expressed, do you agree with the writer? Is there potential bias to the 'facts' or statistics behind an article?

ASSIGNMENTS

In the back of this book, you will find a selection of assignments designed to help you engage with the articles you have been reading and to explore your own opinions. Some tasks will take longer than others and there is a mixture of design, writing and research-based activities that you can complete alone or in a group.

FURTHER RESEARCH

At the end of each article we have listed its source and a website that you can visit if you would like to conduct your own research. Please remember to critically evaluate any sources that you consult and consider whether the information you are viewing is accurate and unbiased.

Useful Websites

www.barnardos.org.uk

www.bhscp.org.uk

www.birmingham.ac.uk

www.childandfamilyblog.com

www.childrenssociety.org.uk

www.counselling-directory.org.uk

www.dailyrecord.co.uk

www.forwarduk.org.uk

www.fullfact.org

www.healthforteens.co.uk

www.iicsa.org.uk

www.independent.co.uk

www.inews.co.uk

www.northamptonchron.co.uk

www.nspcc.org.uk

www.ons.gov.uk

www.safeguarding.network

www.saferinternet.org.uk

www.theconversation.com

www.theguardian.com

www.themaggieoliverfoundation.com

www.thinkuknow.co.uk

www.who.int

Chapter 1

What is Abuse?

What is child abuse?

Child abuse is when anyone who is under the age of 18 is being either intentionally harmed, or not looked after properly. Abuse can be by an adult, or by another child. It may happen over a long period of time, or be a one off. There isn't a legal definition of child abuse, but there are laws in place to protect children and adults who suffered abuse in childhood.

The four main types of abuse are: neglect, physical, emotional and sexual. There are many different forms of abuse discussed in this book, but here we will give a quick breakdown of the main four.

Neglect

Neglect is the failure to meet a child's basic needs by their parent or guardian. This can be psychologically or physically. Neglect may include:

♦ not providing adequate food, clothing or shelter

♦ not allowing medical care or treatment

♦ not protecting a child from physical and emotional harm or danger

♦ inadequate access to education

♦ inadequate supervision (including being left at home alone)

Unlike other forms of abuse, neglect can be intentional or unintentional - some families need more support to prevent neglect from happening.

Physical abuse

Physical abuse is causing physical harm to a child on purpose. Physical abuse may include:

♦ Hitting, slapping or shaking

♦ burning or scalding

♦ physical discipline

♦ misusing medication or fabricating or inducing illness

Emotional abuse

Emotional abuse can happen in many different ways. Although a single incident may be abuse, commonly it is a pattern of behaviour over a period of time. Some forms of emotional abuse can include:

♦ being made to feel frightened or in danger

♦ being made to feel inadequate, worthless or unloved

♦ being made to feel shamed or humiliated

♦ witnessing the abuse of others

♦ bullying (including online)

Sexual abuse

Sexual abuse is when a child is forced or enticed to take part in sexual activities. Sometimes a child may not realise that they are experiencing sexual abuse as they have been groomed by the perpetrator. Sexual abuse can be committed by men and women as well as by other children. Sexual abuse can include:

♦ grooming a child in preparation of abuse (including via the internet)

♦ encouraging a child to behave in a sexually inappropriate way

♦ encouraging or coercing a child to engage in or watch sexual activities, including sexual images or videos

♦ encouraging or coercing a child to make sexual images or videos

If you or anyone you know has been abused, or is suffering abuse right now, there is help out there. Speak to a trusted adult, or one of the charities or organisations who will help you. There is a list of organisations who can help on page 39 of this book.

Child abuse in England and Wales

Child abuse is an appalling crime against some of the most vulnerable in society. It is something that is not often discussed or well understood, and there has been a lack of complete statistics. For the first time, we have compiled a range of indicators from different data sources to enable better understanding of the extent and circumstances of child abuse. Our statistics on abuse experienced in childhood in England and Wales include data on sexual abuse, physical abuse, emotional abuse and neglect. The release also includes statistics on child abuse and the criminal justice system.

◆ The Crime Survey for England and Wales (CSEW) estimated that one in five adults aged 18 to 74 years experienced at least one form of child abuse, whether emotional abuse, physical abuse, sexual abuse, or witnessing domestic violence or abuse, before the age of 16 years (8.5 million people).

◆ In addition, an estimated 1 in 100 adults aged 18 to 74 years experienced physical neglect before the age of 16 years (481,000 people); this includes not being taken care of or not having enough food, shelter or clothing, but it does not cover all types of neglect.

◆ An estimated 3.1 million adults aged 18 to 74 years were victims of sexual abuse before the age of 16 years; this includes abuse by both adult and child perpetrators.

◆ Prevalence was higher for females than males for each type of abuse, with the exception of physical abuse where there was no difference.

◆ Many cases of child abuse remain hidden and do not enter the criminal justice system; around one in seven adults who called the National Association for People Abused in Childhood's (NAPAC's) helpline had not told anyone about their abuse before.

◆ It is possible to identify around 227,500 child abuse offences recorded by the police in the year ending March 2019 of which around 1 in 25 (4%) resulted in a charge or summons.

◆ While not all cases continue through the criminal justice system, almost four in five of child abuse-flagged Crown Prosecution Service (CPS) prosecutions were successful in securing a conviction in the year ending March 2019 (79%).

◆ Childline delivered 19,847 counselling sessions to children in the UK where abuse was the primary concern in the year ending March 2019; sexual abuse accounted for nearly half (45%) of these and has become the most common type of abuse counselled by Childline in recent years.

◆ At 31 March 2019, 52,260 children in England were the subject of a child protection plan (CPP) and 2,820 children in Wales were on the child protection register (CPR) because of experience or risk of abuse or neglect; neglect was the most common category of abuse in England and emotional abuse was the most common in Wales.

◆ At 31 March 2019, 49,570 children in England and 4,810 children in Wales were looked after by their local authority because of experience or risk of abuse or neglect.

◆ Around half of adults (52%) who experienced abuse before the age of 16 years also experienced domestic abuse later in life, compared with 13% of those who did not experience abuse before the age of 16 years.

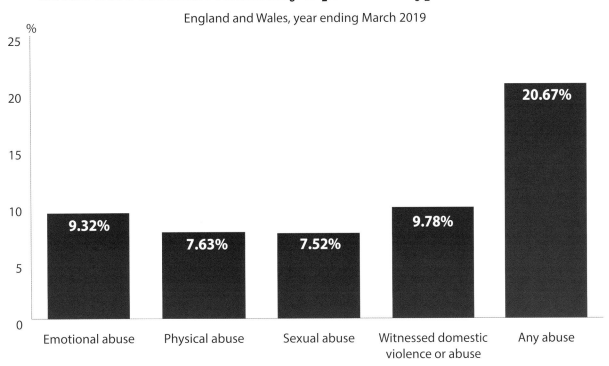

Figure 1: Witnessing domestic violence or abuse and emotional abuse were the most commonly experienced types of child abuse

England and Wales, year ending March 2019

%

- Emotional abuse: **9.32%**
- Physical abuse: **7.63%**
- Sexual abuse: **7.52%**
- Witnessed domestic violence or abuse: **9.78%**
- Any abuse: **20.67%**

Notes:
1. "Don't know or can't remember" and "Don't wish to answer" responses have been excluded.
2. "Any abuse" includes respondents who said they experienced emotional abuse, physical abuse, sexual abuse, or said they witnessed domestic violence or abuse in the home.
3. "Any abuse" will not be the sum of the different types of abuse, as some victims may be included in multiple categories as they can experience more than one type of abuse.
4. "Emotional abuse" was referred to as "psychological abuse" in previous publications.
5. "Sexual abuse" includes rape or assault by penetration (including attempts), other contact sexual abuse, and non-contact sexual abuse.

Source: Office for National Statistics – Crime Survey for England and Wales

Statistician's comment

'Child abuse is an appalling crime against some of the most vulnerable in society, but it is also something that is little discussed or understood. Today's release is ONS's first attempt to fill an important evidence gap on this critical issue.

'Measuring the extent and nature of child abuse is difficult because it is usually hidden from view and comes in many forms. Bringing data together from different sources helps us better understand both the nature of child abuse and the potential demand on support services.'

Alexa Bradley, Centre for Crime and Justice, Office for National Statistics.

What do we know about the prevalence of child abuse?

There is no source providing the current prevalence of abuse during childhood. The Crime Survey for England and Wales (CSEW) provides the best available indicator of prevalence by measuring the prevalence of adults who experienced abuse before the age of 16 years.

The CSEW provides an underestimate of child abuse as abuse against 16- and 17-year-olds is not included. Abuse perpetrated by children aged under 16 years is only included for sexual abuse.

In the year ending March 2019, the CSEW estimated that approximately 8.5 million adults aged 18 to 74 years experienced abuse before the age of 16 years. This is equivalent to 20.7% of the population aged 18 to 74 years.

Just under half of victims experienced more than one type of abuse

Around 4 in 10 of these adults (44%) experienced more than one of emotional abuse, physical abuse, sexual abuse, or witnessing domestic violence or abuse. This proportion is higher for women than men, at 46% compared with 41%.

Women were more likely than men to have experienced abuse before the age of 16 years

Around one in four women (25%; 5.1 million) and around one in six men (16%; 3.3 million) experienced abuse before the age of 16 years.

Prevalence was higher for females than males for each type of abuse, with the exception of physical abuse where there was no difference.

What is often a hidden crime can have an impact later in life

Around half of adults (52%) who experienced abuse before the age of 16 years also experienced domestic abuse later in life, compared with 13% of those who did not experience abuse before the age of 16 years.

The CSEW defines domestic abuse as occurring since the age of 16 years, and it includes sexual abuse, non-sexual abuse and stalking by a partner or family member.

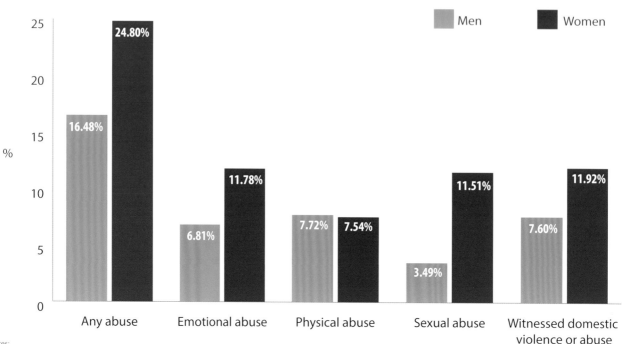

Figure 2: Experience of sexual abuse before the age 16 years showed the greatest difference between men and women

England and Wales, year ending March 2019

Men ▪ Women

- Any abuse: Men 16.48%, Women 24.80%
- Emotional abuse: Men 6.81%, Women 11.78%
- Physical abuse: Men 7.72%, Women 7.54%
- Sexual abuse: Men 3.49%, Women 11.51%
- Witnessed domestic violence or abuse: Men 7.60%, Women 11.92%

Notes:
1. "Any abuse" includes respondents who said they experienced emotional abuse, physical abuse or sexual abuse or said they witnessed domestic violence or abuse in the home.
2. "Emotional abuse" was referred to as "psychological abuse" in previous publications.
3. "Sexual abuse" includes rape or assault by penetration (including attempts), other contact sexual abuse, and non-contact sexual abuse.

Source: Office for National Statistics – Crime Survey for England and Wales

Glossary

Child

A child is defined as anyone who has not yet reached their 18th birthday. The fact that a child has reached 16 years of age; is living independently; is in further education; is a member of the armed forces; is in hospital; or is in custody in the secure estate does not change their status or entitlements to services or protection.

Child abuse

There is not a specific offence of child abuse in law, but practitioners have come to define child abuse based on the laws designed to protect children from harm. Child abuse is any form of maltreatment of a child. Somebody may abuse or neglect a child by inflicting harm, or by failing to act to prevent harm. Children may be abused in a family or in an institutional or community setting by those known to them or, more rarely, by others. Abuse can take place wholly online, or technology may be used to facilitate offline abuse. Children may be abused by an adult or adults, or another child or children.

Child emotional abuse

Child emotional abuse is the persistent emotional maltreatment of a child that causes severe and persistent adverse effects on the child's emotional development. It may involve conveying to a child that they are worthless, unloved, inadequate or valued only insofar as they meet the needs of another person. It may include not giving the child opportunities to express their views, deliberately silencing them or 'making fun' of what they say or how they communicate. It may feature age or developmentally inappropriate expectations being imposed on children. It may involve seeing or hearing the ill-treatment of another. It may involve serious bullying (including cyberbullying), causing children frequently to feel frightened or in danger, or the exploitation or corruption of children. Some level of emotional abuse is involved in all types of maltreatment of a child, but it may occur alone. A child may be emotionally abused by an adult or adults or by another child or children.

Child neglect

Child neglect is the persistent failure to meet a child's basic physical and/or psychological needs, likely to result in the serious impairment of the child's health or development. Neglect may occur during pregnancy as a result of maternal substance abuse. Once a child is born, neglect may involve a parent or carer failing to:

◆ provide adequate food, clothing and shelter (including exclusion from home or abandonment)

◆ protect from physical and emotional harm or danger

◆ ensure adequate supervision (including the use of inadequate care-givers)

◆ ensure access to appropriate medical care or treatment

It may also include neglect of, or unresponsiveness to, a child's basic emotional needs.

Child physical abuse

Child physical abuse is the non-accidental infliction of physical force on a child. This may involve hitting, shaking, throwing, poisoning, burning or scalding, drowning, suffocating, or otherwise causing physical harm to a child. Physical harm may also be caused when a parent or carer fabricates the symptoms of, or deliberately induces, illness in a child. Physical abuse may or may not result in physical injury. A child may be physically abused by an adult or adults or by another child or children.

Child sexual abuse

Child sexual abuse is forcing or enticing a child or young person to take part in sexual activities, not necessarily involving a high level of violence, whether or not the child is aware of what is happening. The activities may involve physical contact, including assault by penetration (for example, rape or oral sex) or non-penetrative acts (for example, masturbation, kissing, rubbing and touching outside of clothing). They may also include non-contact activities, such as involving children in looking at, or in the production of, sexual images, watching sexual activities, encouraging children to behave in sexually inappropriate ways, or grooming a child in preparation for abuse (including via the internet). Sexual abuse is not solely perpetrated by adult males. Women can also commit acts of sexual abuse, as can other children.

Child sexual exploitation

Child sexual exploitation is a form of child sexual abuse where an individual or group takes advantage of an imbalance of power to coerce, manipulate, or deceive a child or young person under the age of 18 years into sexual activity in exchange for something the victim needs or wants and/or for the financial advantage or increased status of the perpetrator or facilitator. The victim may have been sexually exploited even if the sexual activity appears consensual. Child sexual exploitation does not always involve physical contact; it can also occur through the use of technology.

5 March 2020

What is childhood sexual abuse?

*Trigger warning. Please be aware that the following information may be difficult to read and may affect you. If you are a survivor reading this please make sure you take care of yourself and ensure you have someone you can talk about the impact it has on you.

CSE (child sexual exploitation), or CSA (child sexual abuse) both happen when a child or a young person is encouraged or forced to take part in sexual activity. The abuser may give the child presents, money, alcohol or simply attention as part of the grooming process in order to gain the child's trust and draw them in.

People who commit CSE often 'groom' their victims in order to gain their trust. Later, when the behaviour of the abuser starts to change, many children are too frightened to come forward. Violence, coercion and intimidation are often part of CSE as many perpetrators target the most vulnerable of children. This vulnerability is often due to economic or personal circumstances that leave young people with few choices.

Sometimes, children don't realise they are being abused. This might lead them to suffer in silence for years without talking to anyone about what is happening. It can happen to both boys and girls from all backgrounds and communities, right across the UK.

Child sexual exploitation is NEVER the young person's fault, even if they feel that they have 'agreed' to the sexual activity.

It is acknowledged that childhood sexual abuse happens a lot more frequently than people would have believed, or have wanted to believe in the past. The most up to date data currently in the UK comes from the ONS Time Survey 2016, which attest that 7% of the population experienced sexual assault in childhood. To put this is context – less people have diabetes in the UK!

Some survivors are well aware of the trauma they experienced in childhood. They may be troubled by memories of abuse, and they continue to live with the pain, confusion and feelings of loneliness they experienced as a child.

Other survivors may not remember that they have been abused, or they may only remember some experiences of abuse or not be sure at all. They may not understand or acknowledge that what they experienced was abuse or neglect.

It is very common for survivors to deny that an experience was abusive, or to minimise the seriousness of the abuse by thinking or saying 'it only happened once' or 'it wasn't so bad'. Many survivors live with symptoms of abuse, such as panic attacks, strange body sensations, inexplicable fears and anxiety, or aches and pains, that they are unable to explain. Their body remembers what happens to them, and they relive the emotions and feelings associated with abuse over and over again – but many survivors don't connect these symptoms to their childhood abuse.

You may not be sure if you were sexually abused or not so we have listed some of the things that have happened to people who we've worked with as a guideline. Please note this is not comprehensive and if you are in any doubt about whether you were sexually abused as a child please feel free to get in touch or discuss with a healthcare professional.

Sexual abuse involves an abuse of power – the abuser being an adult or an older child. Sexual abuse also involves an abuse of trust.

Childhood sexual abuse can include (but is not limited to) the following:

♦ Being cuddled or kissed in a way that made you feel uncomfortable.

♦ Being bathed or cleaned in a way that made you feel uncomfortable.

♦ Having to look at other people's genitals.

♦ Having to touch other people's genitals.

♦ Having your own breasts or genitals touched.

♦ Having to pose for photographs or videos of a sexual nature.

♦ Being shown films and/or having to listen to sexual talk.

♦ Having your vagina or anus penetrated by a penis, finger or object.

Possible forms of child sexual exploitation

Inappropriate relationships

Inappropriate relationships often involve one perpetrator with power or control over a young person. Maybe this is because they are physically stronger, older or in a position of authority/care.

Older adult exploitation (sometimes called the 'boyfriend' model)

Sometimes an offender is several years older and 'befriends' (or grooms) the young person by exploiting their vulnerabilities. The child may initially feel they are in a positive and rewarding relationship with the adult.

Due to power imbalances and control issues, young people can become isolated and more and more dependent on the 'boyfriend', often being coerced or forced into sex with them and their associates.

Trafficking

Young people are sometimes passed by adults between locations, whether it be their associates' homes or towns and cities, where they may be forced or coerced into sexual activity, often with multiple people. This is known as trafficking. Young people are sometimes made to recruit other young people to take part.

Sexual bullying

Sexual bullying refers to unwanted pressure from the child's peers to have sexual contact and includes cyberbullying.

Sexual bullying can happen quickly without the forming of a relationship or the grooming process. Incidents may be filmed on mobile phones and circulated. It can occur publicly or involve multiple perpetrators.

Gang and group exploitation

Young people in gangs or groups may be sexually exploited as part of gang initiation or punishment. They may also be encouraged to recruit more children, exposing them to CSE and making it difficult to identify those who control the gang.

Children are often also groomed and befriended by abusers, pretending to be 'friends' or 'boyfriends' before being 'passed around' gangs of predatory abusers. This is often referred to as 'on street grooming'.

Spotting signs

♦ Mood swings – angry, emotional, withdrawn, suicide attempts, depression.

♦ Bruising, scarring on the body.

♦ Receiving gifts.

♦ Staying out late or not returning home.

♦ Secretive and distant towards family and friends.

♦ Skipping education.

♦ Involved in criminal activity.

♦ Education grades dropping.

♦ Sexually transmitted infections.

♦ Pregnancy or miscarriage.

♦ Using alcohol or drugs.

♦ Eating disorders.

♦ Not sleeping, nightmares, anxiety, panic attacks.

♦ Violence or aggression towards parents, siblings or animals.

Why won't a victim come forward?

There are many reasons why a victim won't disclose the abuse they are suffering. It might be that the victim…

♦ Doesn't recognise it as abuse.

♦ Believes the abuser is their boyfriend / thinks it's normal.

♦ Finds it too difficult to talk about.

♦ Thinks the abuser will change.

♦ Feels embarrassed, ashamed, judged, to blame, fears rejection, will become isolated or called a liar.

♦ Becomes emotionally attached to the abuser.

♦ Feels will put themselves and family at risk.

♦ Doesn't know who to tell or trust.

♦ Becomes addicted to drugs or alcohol.

♦ Has committed criminal offences.

♦ Has lost trust in the police, the CPS and the criminal justice system.

♦ Doesn't know where to turn for help and support.

The Maggie Oliver Foundation began its life in June 2019, and is underpinned by the passion of its Founder to support victims of childhood sexual abuse and ensure that the criminal justice system is fit for purpose in supporting them to achieve the justice they deserve.

Our vision is a society where every survivor is treated with dignity, respect and as an equal and valued member of society and we will help every adult survivor who approaches The Foundation by providing support that is consistent, personal and focused on the needs of the individual as we help them on their path to recovery by transforming their personal pain into power.

If you are an adult survivor of sexual abuse and need our help, please self refer in the first instance via help@ themaggieoliverfoundation.com and we will be in touch.

You will be treated with empathy, kindness, compassion, honesty, integrity and human decency.

Emotional abuse

Emotional abuse, sometimes referred to as psychological abuse, is used to describe any type of behaviour that allows someone to gain power and control over another. There are many different types of emotional abuse, all of which gradually undermine the other person's self-respect.

This can occur in any kind of relationship - be it within a couple, a friendship, amongst family members or colleagues. It can happen at any stage in a person's life. Spotting the signs of emotional abuse can be trickier than other more overt types of abuse, which can lead to some people overlooking, ignoring, or dismissing the signs.

If you are on the receiving end of emotional abuse, it can be just as damaging and as upsetting as other forms of abuse. Controlling or coercive behaviour are both considered serious crimes.

In this article, we'll explore how emotional abuse can make you feel, tackle some of the common myths and misconceptions, and look at how you can find help if you are experiencing emotional abuse.

What is emotional abuse?

Most people know what physical or sexual abuse is, but when it comes to emotional abuse, some people think of it more of a 'grey area'. They might know it has something to do with treating someone else badly, but not be clear on what's actually classed as emotional abuse.

The problem is, unlike with other types of abuse, there are no scars or marks, so emotional abuse can be difficult to identify. But, these behaviours can be incredibly damaging to our mental health and if not dealt with, the torment can continue indefinitely and can have far-reaching effects.

Some people may be hesitant about using the phrase 'emotional abuse' when describing how someone else is treating them. It's important to remember that any behaviour that makes you feel controlled, small, unable to talk or seek help, is abusive.

If someone is stopping you from expressing yourself, is belittling your opinions, is making you doubt events or experiences you know to be true (known as gaslighting), this is abusive behaviour. If you find yourself changing how you act to better accommodate their behaviour, or find yourself feeling scared or anxious about their reactions, this is abusive behaviour.

Types of emotional abuse

There are many different types of abuse and although emotional abuse may occur on its own, you may also face physical or sexual abuse alongside it. There are a variety of types of behaviour that could be classed as emotional abuse, which include:

Intimidation or threats. This is often done to make a person feel small and to stop them from standing up for themselves. This could be things like shouting, acting aggressively or making you feel scared.

Criticism. This could be things like name-calling or making unpleasant, belittling comments. It can also include refusing to acknowledge your successes, belittling your strengths or accomplishments. This can heavily affect your self-esteem and self-confidence.

Undermining. This might include things like dismissing your opinion or disputing your version of events (a form of gaslighting) so that you begin to doubt yourself. They might tell you that you're being oversensitive if you get upset.

Making you feel guilty. This can range from emotional blackmail to ignoring you, by way of manipulation. Or they may suddenly act really nice towards you after being cruel - making you feel sorry for them.

Name-calling. They may use derogatory names or phrases when speaking with you, put you down in conversations, or say things to make you feel bad about yourself. These hurtful things may be disguised as a 'joke' or played off as sarcasm when questioned.

Different treatment. An emotionally abusive partner, friend or sibling may treat you differently from your siblings, other friends, or family. They may also put you in dangerous situations, try to control you, or put pressure on you to do things that you aren't comfortable with or don't want to do.

Isolation. This can include stopping you from having friends, making you doubt if friends or other family members really care about you, or trying to exclude you from gatherings or events. If your partner constantly requires you to check-in, wants to know where you are, who you are with, or requires proof of where you are or who you are with, these can be further signs of controlling and isolating behaviours.

Withholding affection, sex, or money. This may be as a method of controlling you, trying to make you change your behaviours or opinions.

Signs of emotional abuse in children and teens

Young people may not feel comfortable or able to reach out until they reach a crisis point. For children, they may not understand what is happening to them or that what is happening is wrong.

If you're worried about a child, signs to look out for include:

♦ a lack of confidence or self-assurance

♦ trouble dealing with their emotions

♦ difficulty making (or maintaining) friendships or other relationships, including few or no friends, as well as isolation from their parents

♦ behaviour that is inappropriate or unusual for their age

♦ extreme outbursts or a lack of social skills

For pre-school aged children, signs may also include being overly-affectionate with strangers, seeming wary or anxious, a lack of a close bond with their parents, aggressive or cruel behaviour towards other children or animals.

Emotional abuse is generally about control. Sometimes this is explicit; if you are told when and where you can go out, or whether you can see certain people. Other times, however, it might be more implicit; neglect or withholding affection may seem less abusive than more outwardly aggressive behaviours, but can be just as hurtful.

How do I know if I'm being emotionally abused?

Conflict, arguments and criticism are all healthy ways of interacting with others - but there is a clear difference between this and emotional abuse: the way we feel.

If you're on the receiving end, it can be extremely damaging and upsetting - and this is reflected in the law; The Serious Crime Act 2015. This makes behaviour that is 'controlling or coercive', in an intimate or family relationship, punishable by a prison sentence.

I'm being emotionally abused - what do I do?

If you think you may be experiencing emotional abuse, or are worried that a loved one is being emotionally abused, there are things you can do to help.

Speak out. Telling someone you are being abused means you no longer have to deal with it alone. Anonymous helplines can offer a safe, judgement-free place to talk through any worries or concerns if you feel nervous or unsure about speaking to anyone in-person, or aren't sure if you are ready to open up to friends or family.

Keep records. Keeping a diary of what is happening to you can help to remind you of the scale and scope of the emotional abuse you are experiencing. When abusers are being nice, it can be easy to forget, overlook, or convince ourselves that past events 'weren't that bad' or must have become overblown in our memories. Keeping a diary of events and how they made you feel can help you to put their behaviour in perspective.

Prioritise you. Make your mental and physical health a priority, and start taking care of your needs rather than worrying about pleasing others. Practising self-care, ensuring you get enough sleep, and eating balanced, regular meals can all help you to feel more able to deal with day-to-day stress and challenges that may arise.

Stop blaming yourself. People who have been emotionally abused may believe it is their fault, that they have done something to make them 'deserve' what is happening, or that something is wrong with them. Abuse is never ok. You are not the problem. Recognising that you are worthy of having your own opinions, feeling safe, and being able to express yourself can be the first step towards escaping the cycle of self-blame and guilt, and acknowledging that you are not to blame.

Work on an exit plan. If the person who is being emotionally abusive, be they your partner, family member, or friend, has no intention of changing or working towards fixing problem behaviours, creating an exit plan may be one way to help you escape the cycle of abuse. Emotional abuse can take a toll, mentally and physically. If things become too much, you may need to take steps to remove yourself safely from the relationship.

As each situation is different and unique, it may be best to discuss your thoughts and plans with a trusted friend, family member, counsellor, or to speak with a helpline for advice and guidance on your next steps.

Worried about someone? Be supportive. If you are worried someone else may be experiencing emotional abuse, try to talk with them. Let them know that you care, that people do love and appreciate them, and if they need to talk, they can reach out to you (or helplines or someone else, if you do not feel comfortable or confident).

Am I emotionally abusive?

Recognising that your behaviour may be emotionally abusive can be tough. Emotional abusers may not actively be aware that they are being abusive, however, it is possible to pick up habits, fall into negative patterns, or to even be influenced by the relationships and behaviours we have seen around us that may not be healthy.

Signs to look out for can include:

You have trouble accepting that there are two sides to an argument. Apologising or recognising that you may have been wrong or have overreacted can be tough, but in healthy relationships, couples apologise and look at ways to improve and move forward together. If you struggle to accept your role or contribution in an argument, it can be a warning sign.

Has your partner become a people pleaser? If their behaviour has changed, it could be worth considering why they are now acting this way, and if there is anything in your relationship that may be contributing to this. Some people who have experienced emotional abuse may try to please others in an attempt to feel more secure, as their self-esteem may have been impacted.

You use 'silent treatment' frequently. Trying to control others and get your own way doesn't just mean screaming, shouting, or saying cruel or hurtful things. Refusing to talk about what has upset you and keeping your partner in suspense of what will happen can be ways of controlling others.

Taking a step back and returning to the conversation can be a good way to avoid heated arguments or saying things you may regret, but if you are shutting down the conversation or refusing to discuss things, these can be warning signs.

You minimise or ignore ongoing issues. It can be tempting to downplay things when they are going wrong,

but repeatedly brushing them off, refusing to face them, or denying that anything is wrong can create a sense of frustration, may leave your partner feeling unable to speak with you, or could border on gaslighting behaviour.

You put them down, instead of helping build them up. Making someone else feel or look bad to put yourself in a better light or to make yourself feel better is never ok. This can be a sign that you may have self-esteem issues.

Part of being in a healthy partnership is supporting and contributing towards each other's well-being. This could be through offering help and supportive words through new projects or hobbies, career moves, or acknowledging each other's skills or successes. Being kind, rather than looking good, as well as listening and behaving in a way that shows love are care are all key ways of helping to build up self-esteem.

If you are worried about your relationship, or are concerned that you may need help and support learning new ways to cope with stress, anger, anxiety, or unhealthy behaviours, working with a counsellor or therapist could help.

Common misconceptions surrounding emotional abuse

There are a number of myths and misconceptions that surround emotional abuse. For instance, some people believe that emotional abuse is merely another term for 'verbal abuse'. It is true that emotional abuse does often include verbal abuse, but it can involve non-verbal and other non-physical forms of abuse. For example, being ignored.

Some common misconceptions include:

♦ 'Emotional abuse only happens in romantic relationships' - when we think of emotional abuse, many people will picture a couple or a parent and child scenario. Whilst emotional abuse is commonly a part of domestic violence and child abuse, there are many other relationships that be affected by emotional abuse. These can include friendships and working relationships, too.

♦ 'Emotional abuse only affects women' - while the majority of abuse victims (particularly in a domestic setting) are women, all forms of abuse can also happen to men and non-binary individuals too.

People with a disability can also be vulnerable to emotional abuse. Sadly, in some cases, a person's caregiver and abuser are one and the same. These situations are especially risky, since the person with the disability may be dependent on their caregiver for basic needs.

'At the time, I didn't think Mike was treating me badly. He was giving me everything I'd ever wanted and that I'd never had before – love, acceptance, happiness, support, understanding. The problem was that I didn't get any of that without emotional blackmail, mind games and pressure that resulted in sexual abuse.'

- Phil shares his story, fighting for the rights of other male abuse victims.

What are the effects of emotional abuse?

Experiencing abuse of any kind can lead to a number of different emotions. There is no right or wrong way to feel. You may experience some (or all) of the following:

- depression or anxiety
- increased isolation from friends and family
- fearful or agitated behaviour
- lower self-esteem and self-confidence
- addiction to alcohol or drugs
- escapist behaviour

In children, emotional abuse can lead to behavioural, emotional development, and mental health problems. This can include self-harming behaviour, trouble with language development, difficulty in forming and maintaining healthy relationships. They may be more likely to experience depression, have trouble expressing and controlling their emotions, may lack confidence, or develop risky behaviours (such as bullying, stealing, or running away).

Emotional abuse can damage a person's confidence so that they feel worthless and find it hard to make or keep other relationships. Secrecy and shame usually maintain abuse.

'One of the hardest things about emotional abuse is that, through a campaign of blame, undermining, criticism and gaslighting, it can cause you to lose trust in yourself.'

- Counsellor Jo Baker.

You mustn't lose trust in yourself. Your feelings may have been frequently invalidated or dismissed and you may have suppressed your feelings for believing that they are wrong. But you must remember that the person who has taken control of your emotions has done so wrongly.

You are not worth less than other people and you can be happy and confident again.

When is the right time to seek help?

If your behaviour starts to change and you are no longer able to find satisfaction in your work or social life, it is time to consider seeking help.

If people you trust express concern about you or your relationship, one of the best things you can do is talk to them about what's going on. Talking to someone outside of the situation can help give you a little perspective. They can help you to assess whether this relationship is abusive and whether you would be better without this person in your life.

Emotional abuse can have a damaging effect on you, so it is important to seek help and support to prevent it from becoming entrenched. Learning to care for your own needs and to feel entitled to be confident and respected is a good start to being able to claim your own self-esteem.

'I began meditating again, I prayed and I surrounded myself with personal development resources that I knew would help me reconnect with my true self. Even though I was still living with him, I gradually detached emotionally and mentally. I began seeing everything more clearly.'

- Holly shares how she moved forward from an emotionally abusive relationship.

Finding help and support for emotional abuse

It can be helpful to seek help from a counsellor or therapist in order to help you see a way out and escape from a cycle of powerlessness.

You may not feel comfortable speaking to loved ones about what is going on, or maybe you have, yet they aren't sure of how to help you further. Counselling offers you a safe space to talk, without fear and without judgement. They can listen to you, and help you come to terms with what has happened, and understand your options for moving forward.

If you are no longer in an abusive relationship, but still feel the effects from what the other person put you through, a counsellor can help you come to terms with what has happened and move forward with your life. Trusting new people might feel especially difficult right now - but it will get easier. Finding a counsellor you trust and connect with is particularly important in helping you do this.

Counselling, psychotherapy and CBT all have their place and for many people, it is the beginning of a long, but rewarding journey to a better and more fulfilling way of living by breaking old, unhealthy patterns.

Neglect

Neglect is the most prevalent form of abuse in the UK with half of all children being on child protection plans in England are there because of neglect.

Statistics to the end of 2018 compiled by the NSPCC suggest that half of all children on child protection plans in England are on plans because of concerns about neglect. Research from 2011 (the most recent comprehensive research available) suggests that 1 in 10 children will have experienced neglect (Radford et al, 2011) – i.e. potentially 3 children in every class of 30. Neglect can be life threatening and should be treated with as much urgency as other categories of abuse.

We often intervene too slowly with neglect, sometimes because no single incident acts as a trigger, with concerns usually building up over time. At other times referrals are made to other agencies and perhaps are not taken sufficiently seriously. We need to understand the cumulative effects of neglect and actively review the concerns to understand the level of harm caused.

Definition of neglect:

Neglect is the persistent failure to meet a child's basic physical and/or psychological needs, likely to result in the serious impairment of the child's health or development.

– Keeping Children Safe in Education, 2020

Types of neglect

♦ **Educational** – not ensuring the child receives/attends appropriate education

♦ **Physical** – failure to provide for basic needs, e.g. food, shelter, or ensure safety

♦ **Emotional** – failure to meet a child's need for stimulation or nurture/love. This overlaps with emotional abuse and may involve ignoring, intimidating or humiliating the child.

♦ **Medical** – a failure to ensure a child receives appropriate medical care, including dental care, or ignoring medical advice. It includes the failure of the parent/carer to take their child to appointments.

Neglect should therefore be considered as the most common form of abuse and can have a serious and long-term impact on the child. Children who suffer neglect may also suffer from other forms of abuse as well.

Sometimes it is because parents/carers won't look after their children and sometimes because they are unable to. Neglect may occur during pregnancy as a result of maternal substance misuse.

Neglect may involve the failure of the parent/carer to provide adequate food, clothing and shelter, including the exclusion of the child from the home. It may also be the parent/carer failing to protect a child from emotional harm or danger and/or failing to provide adequate supervision (including the use of inadequate carers).

The failure of the parent/carer to provide access to appropriate medical care or treatment are also considered to be forms of neglect.

Whilst it is the most common form of abuse it is also one of the most difficult to recognise as there is often no single sign and so professionals wait for a pattern of neglect to build up over time. Maintaining a chronology of concerns is therefore key.

Physical indicators of neglect

♦ Constant hunger

♦ Poor personal hygiene

♦ Poor dental health

♦ Skin rashes, lice etc

♦ Constant tiredness

♦ Inadequate and/or dirty ill- fitting clothing

♦ Untreated medical problems

♦ Under/overweight

Behavioural indicators of neglect

♦ Social isolation

♦ Low self-esteem

♦ Frequent lateness or nonattendance at school

♦ Missed medical /dental appointments

♦ Destructive tendencies

♦ Poor relationships with peers

♦ Compulsive stealing/scavenging

Groups vulnerable to neglect

Some vulnerabilities include:

♦ Parents/carers out of the house for prolonged periods

♦ Poverty

♦ Parents/carers with substance/alcohol misuse issues

♦ Parents/carers with mental health issues or disabilities

♦ Children with disabilities

♦ Children being left on their own for prolonged periods or being left in the care of siblings or unsuitable carers

As with all forms of abuse, any child can be a victim of neglect regardless of whether they fit any of the criteria on this list or not.

2020

Physical abuse

Physical abuse is any way of causing deliberate physical harm to a child, including hitting, slapping, punching, shaking, throwing, kicking, poisoning, burning or scalding, biting, scratching, breaking bones, drowning, or suffocating.

Physical abuse also includes making up the symptoms of an illness or deliberately causing a child to become unwell, which can happen by giving the child unnecessary medication. This is known as fabricated or induced illness (FII).

Shaking or hitting babies is a form of physical abuse which can cause abusive head trauma (AHT) and non-accidental head injuries (NAHI).

Effects of physical abuse

Physical abuse can have long-lasting effects on a child.

Many parents shake their baby as an impulsive reaction to crying, and many don't understand the consequences of head shaking. If a baby or infant is shaken or thrown they may suffer abusive head trauma (AHT), also known as shaken baby syndrome, resulting in injuries to the head or brain, eyes, and some other areas, which can lead to long-term disabilities, learning problems, seizures, sight issues or blindness, speech problems, behavioural issues, brain damage or death.

Other consequences of physical abuse on children of all ages include:

◆ Poor mental health, including anxiety and depression

◆ Poor self-esteem

◆ Eating disorders

◆ Self-harm and attempts at suicide

◆ Behaviour issues

◆ Criminal behaviour

◆ Drug and alcohol problems

◆ Issues at school

◆ Trouble eating and/or sleeping properly

◆ Risky sexual behaviour

◆ Difficulties forming relationships in the long term

Signs of physical abuse

Knowing the signs of physical abuse can help give a voice to a child. Any child can experience physical abuse, but some parents and carers might find it difficult to provide a safe and loving home if they are experiencing financial hardship and poverty, isolation, issues with drugs and alcohol, inadequate housing, mental health issues, relationship issues, domestic abuse, or a lack of support.

All children have bumps, trips, and falls, and not all cuts and bruises mean that a child is being physically abused. If a child has repeated or patterned injuries, this needs to be reported. Other signs of physical abuse include:

◆ Bruises (particularly indicative of abuse if observed in infants and immobile children)

◆ Broken or fractured bones, or evidence of old fractures

◆ Burns or scalds, particularly to the feet or the bottom

◆ Lacerations to the body or mouth

◆ Bite marks

◆ Scarring

◆ The effects of poisoning (e.g. vomiting, drowsiness, seizures)

◆ Breathing problems from drowning, suffocation, or poisoning

◆ Head injuries in babies and toddlers may be signalled by the following symptoms: swelling, bruising, fractures, being extremely sleepy, breathing problems, vomiting seizures, being irritable or not feeding properly

◆ Seeming frightened of parents, reluctant to return home after school

◆ Displays frozen watchfulness

◆ Constantly asking in words/actions what will happen next

◆ Shrinks away at the approach of adults

Female genital mutilation

According to the World Health Organisation, female genital mutilation (FGM) comprises 'all procedures involving partial or total removal of the external female genitalia or other injury to the female genital organs for non-medical reasons.' A harmful practice with no health benefits, FGM can cause long-lasting physical, emotional and psychological trauma; and in some cases, death.

Female genital mutilation is classified into four major types:

Type 1– Clitoridectomy: partial or total removal of the clitoris (a small, sensitive and erectile part of the female genitals) and, in very rare cases, only the prepuce (the fold of skin surrounding the clitoris).

Type 2 – Excision: partial or total removal of the clitoris and the labia minora, with or without excision of the labia majora (the labia are 'the lips' that surround the vagina).

Type 3 – Infibulation: narrowing of the vaginal opening through the creation of a covering seal. The seal is formed by cutting and repositioning the inner, or outer, labia, with or without removal of the clitoris.

Type 4 – Other: all other harmful procedures to the female genitalia for non-medical purposes, e.g. pricking, piercing, incising, scraping and cauterizing the genital area.

FGM in numbers

137,000
Women and girls are living with the consquences of FGM in the UK

200 million
Women and girls worldwide have undergone FGM

Where does FGM happen?

Many cultures have different reasons for continuing FGM. From upholding the status of the community to maintaining her virginity, marriageability and bride price. From enhancing her beauty to increasing her husband's sexual pleasure. These cultural, economic and religious justifications assume FGM benefits the girl as she transitions to womanhood.

Global Female Genital Mutilation (FGM) Prevalence Map
(Types 1-3)

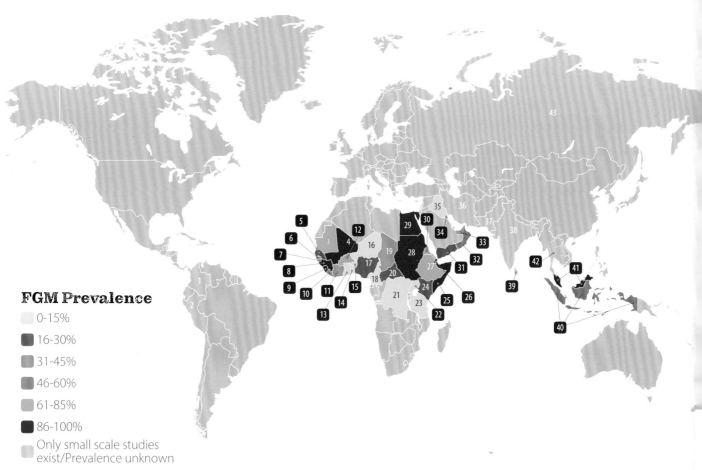

FGM Prevalence

- 0-15%
- 16-30%
- 31-45%
- 46-60%
- 61-85%
- 86-100%
- Only small scale studies exist/Prevalence unknown

Source: FORWARD. Note: All map data courtesy of: WHO, DHS, MICS and Unicef and represents women 15-49 years old, thanks to National FGM Centre.

Myths and facts about FGM

Myth 1: An uncut woman will become promiscuous ('sleep around') and have an uncontrollable sexual appetite.

Fact 1: FGM makes no difference to a woman's sexual appetite but can stop her from enjoying sex. Sexual desire mainly arises from hormones secreted by glands in the brain. Women should be able to choose what level of sexual activity is right for them personally. Some women like to wait to have sex until they are married, some feel ready earlier. So long as sexual activity is safe and respectful, all that matters is that women do what they feel is right.

Myth 2: If the clitoris is not cut, it will harm the husband during intercourse.

Fact 2: The clitoris gives a woman sexual pleasure and does not cause any harm to her or her husband.

Myth 3: If a woman does not undergo FGM, her genitals will smell.

Fact 3: FGM will not make the vagina any more hygienic. In fact, Type 3 FGM can make the vagina less hygienic.

Our approach to ending FGM

Engaging the community

FORWARD's work with affected communities safeguards girls at risk of FGM and supports women living with the consequences – in Africa and practising migrant communities in the UK and Europe. We engage directly with women and men in communities to raise awareness of the risks of FGM. We support them through training and confidence building – which enable them to advocate for change in their communities.

Female genital mutilation is sometimes referred to with other terms like female circumcision and female genital cutting. We use 'female genital mutilation', because we believe it most accurately describes the experience and effects of FGM on women and girls. 'Mutilation' emphasises the severity of the practice and abuse of women and girls' human rights.

> **'The attitude towards FGM has changed dramatically over the years, mostly for the better... the more we address this issue, the more the community feels empowered – and not like victims.'**
>
> Bristol community engagement participant, 2018

Working with professionals

We train and support professionals engaging with affected communities – by raising awareness of the issues and by building their confidence to support at-risk communities in ways respectful of local cultures. We advocate and campaign for change at policy-level in the UK, EU and Africa.

Building partnerships

We develop strategic partnerships with community-based organisations, to develop their technical capacity, and build local support networks for African women and girls.

> **FACT: The Tanzania 2016 Demographic Health Survey reported a 5% reduction in the prevalence of FGM over 5 years. Our continuing work in this region contributes to positive change for young girls at risk of FGM.**

Countries

1.	Colombia	22.	Uganda
2.	Peru	23.	Tanzania
3.	Mauritania	24.	Kenya
4.	Mali	25.	Somalia
5.	Senegal	26.	Djibouti
6.	The Gambia	27.	Ethiopia
7.	Guinea Bissau	28.	Sudan
8.	Guinea	29.	Egypt
9.	Sierra Leone	30.	Eritrea
10.	Liberia	31.	Yemen
11.	Cote D'ivoire	32.	Oman
12.	Burkina Faso	33.	United Arab Emirates
13.	Ghana	34.	Kuwait
14.	Togo	35.	Iraq
15.	Benin	36.	Iran
16.	Niger	37.	Pakistan
17.	Nigeria	38.	India
18.	Cameroon	39.	Sri Lanka
19.	Chad	40.	Indonesia
20.	Central African Republic	41.	Malaysia
21.	Democratic Republic of the Congo	42.	Thailand
		43.	Russia

www.who.int

www.forwarduk.org.uk

Forced marriage: Just the facts

Forced marriage is a crime in Great Britain.

What is a forced marriage?

A forced marriage is where one or both people consent to marriage after pressure and/or abuse is used.

Any person may be forced into a marriage, including people of all ages, genders, ethnicities and religions.

In the UK, forced marriage is seen to be a form of violence against men and women, and is classed as domestic abuse and child abuse, which both violate an individual's human rights.

Forced marriage is illegal in the UK, and that includes taking someone overseas and forcing them to marry, whether the marriage takes place or not, and marrying someone who lacks the mental capacity to consent to the marriage.

The pressure that is put on people to marry can take different forms:

- Physical: including threats, actual physical violence and sexual violence

- Emotional and psychological: for example, when someone is made to feel like they're bringing shame on their family

- Financial abuse: including taking away their wages or not giving them any money

Is forced marriage different to arranged marriage?

An arranged marriage is NOT the same as a forced marriage.

In an arranged marriage, both parties consent and are free to choose whether they enter a marriage or not, with parents respecting their wishes.

Why do forced marriages happen?

Forced marriages can happen for a number of reasons, including:

- The family doesn't approve of their child's sexuality

- The family doesn't approve of their child's existing relationship or doesn't want them to have a relationship

- To help family claims for citizenship or residency

- To maintain a family's reputation or honour

- The family think it's important as part of their culture or religion

- Financial gain or to make sure the family's wealth stays within the family

- The family feel pressured by other family members to follow traditions

- To honour a long standing family commitment

- To control unwanted behaviour

- To reduce the stigma of a disability

This list of reasons is not exhaustive and there are many other reasons why children and other individuals are forced into marriage. None of these reasons are okay and no one should be forced into marrying someone.

Who to contact if you are at risk

Raising a concern can be a scary thing to do, but there are ways that you can be protected. School holidays are often an ideal time for forced marriages to take place, as unfortunately a lot of the time an individual believes that they are going on a holiday and are not aware of what is going to happen if they are taken out of the country.

If you or anyone you know think they are at risk of being forced into a marriage, it's important that you tell a trusted adult such as a teacher, school nurse or GP as soon as possible.

If you can't talk to a trusted adult, you can still access support for your concerns, via ChatHealth, Childline, or your local police on 101. In an emergency, you must call the police on 999.

What to do if you are travelling abroad and are worried about forced marriage

If you are worried that a family member or someone else is taking you out of the country where you will be forced into marriage it is important that you seek help.

You can contact services like Childline or the Forced Marriage Unit for advice if you are concerned. There are a number of things that can be done to help protect you.

♦ Leave as many details with a trusted friend, adult or the Forced Marriage Unit as possible including:

♦ Name and date of birth as shown on passport

♦ Passport number (with date and place of issue)

♦ Overseas contact details and address of where you'll be staying

♦ Number of secret mobile taken overseas

♦ Address and telephone number (including mobile) in the UK

♦ A recent photograph

♦ Contact details of a trusted third party in the UK

♦ Parents' names and address(es)

♦ Departure and expected return date (copies of tickets if possible)

♦ Names of those you are travelling with

♦ Names of family members remaining in the UK

♦ Any other useful information such as any secret code words

♦ Apply for a Forced Marriage Protection Order - this is a legal document that can stop you being taken out of the country and can also help to bring you back to the UK if you have been taken out of the country

♦ Speak to security staff at the airport that you are travelling from. Many airport bathrooms have posters in the toilets offering help and support with advice on what to do. Placing a metal spoon in your underwear can also alert airport staff, however this is not always recommended if you're under the age of 17 as an adult will have to advocate for you

♦ Have contact information for the forced marriage unit of the British Embassy in case you need help whilst abroad

REMEMBER: NO ONE HAS THE RIGHT TO FORCE YOU INTO A MARRIAGE. HELP IS AVAILABLE

30 July 2020

Child marriage is still legal in the UK. At last, the first step has been taken to ban it

Not many Britons know that in England and Wales, 16- and 17-year-olds can marry with parental 'consent'. For 'consent' read 'coercion'.

By Yasmin Alibhai-Brown

Periodically, the small screen makes such a massive impact on viewers it spurs political action and social reform. Did you watch Honour on ITV last week? Please do, if you didn't.

The two-parter was based on the truly tragic, brief life of Banaz Mahmod, a British-Kurdish girl who was forced to marry at the age of 17.

Her older husband allegedly abused her until she fled and soon after, fell in love with Rahmat Sulemani, a fellow Kurd. The couple were harassed and threatened. They approached the police five times for help and no action was taken. For seeking safety and happiness, in 2006, her father and other relatives organised her execution.

Male relatives raped and tortured Banaz before strangling her. Caroline Goode, a good cop, located Banaz's body and nailed the killers.

Kurdish contacts tell me the men are unrepentant. Heartbroken Sulemani killed himself in 2016. Her older sister had escaped earlier and is still in hiding. Their younger sister, Payzee, was 16 when she, too, was made to marry a much older groom.

She told *The Observer* recently: 'It felt like I was for sale.' Now she is one of the spokespeople of the Iranian and Kurdish Women's Rights Organisation, which campaigns against child marriages in the UK.

Not many Britons know that in England and Wales, 16- and 17-year-olds can marry with parental 'consent'. For 'consent', read 'coercion'.

Forced marriages were criminalised in 2014, child marriages were not. Way back in 2004, the Labour MP Anne Cryer agitated for action. It came to nothing. Data from the Office of National Statistics show that between 2006 and 2016, 3,354 marriages involving children aged 16 to 17 were registered in England and Wales.

No figures are available for unregistered religious or 'community' nuptials.

I knew three Bangladeshi sisters who went through these ceremonies when they were young teens. When they turned 18, they bolted, returned to education and are flourishing. The eldest helped the siblings to get away and claim back their lives.

In 2018, a third of the cases dealt with by the Forced Marriage Unit involved under-18s; some boys, mostly girls.

This domestic grooming, sexual violence and trafficking has been going on for decades. In 1982, Sameem Ali, who is from Glasgow, was taken to Pakistan and forced to marry a man when she was just 13. At 14 she was pregnant. The child gave birth to a child. She has since written a painfully honest book about her experiences, titled *Belonging*.

She survived, got divorced, found a good man, success and personal power. Mothers, who themselves were conditioned from childhood, are complicit in these terrible crimes against their own children. Ali's was, so too the mother of Banaz and the three Bangla escapees.

In 2020, gender equality and autonomy is guaranteed by law and is a fundamental British value, yet some (obviously not all) South Asian, Turkish, Kurdish, Middle Eastern and North African families still follow ignominious 'honour' codes that stipulate females have no will, no choice, no human rights, no worth. All they can and must do is acquiesce to the patriarchy. People in these hermetic enclaves do not tolerate any encroachment of their hard cultural borders.

Their young girls and women live in an open society but are not free. Those who try to fly free are captured, caged and made to submit. It is all unspeakably cruel. And, in the case of these marriages at 16 and 17, within the law. Staggering. Are these females not human? Do they not bleed? They miss out on education and employment and can never be independent.

As Human Rights Watch points out: 'In 2014, the UK government hosted the high-profile Girl Summit, designed to boost – and pledging UK leadership for – global efforts to end child marriage and female genital mutilation. But in the years since, the UK government not only failed to ban child marriage at home – it actually blocked an earlier effort to do so.'

Pauline Latham is a Tory and hardline Brexiter whose voting record makes this left-winger shudder. But she has pushed persistently over many years for child marriages to be criminalised when too many other politicians were either indifferent or inert.

Now Labour's Sarah Champion and others are co-operating with Latham to make the issue a cross-party priority. On 6 October, she successfully introduced a Bill under the 10-minute rule, which would make 18 the legal age for marriage with no exceptions and revoke the parental consent law. The second reading will be in November.

Looks as if we will get this new law. It should be dedicated to beautiful, spirited Banaz.

7 October 2020

What is sexual grooming?

Grooming is a process offenders use to abuse and exploit children. It can happen online and in person. Learning more about grooming can help you spots signs and know what to do if you have concerns.

Grooming can happen in online spaces as well as in person, by a stranger or someone known. It involves the offender building a relationship with a child, and sometimes with their wider family, gaining their trust and a position of power over the child, in preparation for abuse. The process of grooming can take place in a matter of minutes, over one conversation, or over long periods of time, in some cases, years.

Sexual grooming refers to grooming where the offender aims to sexually abuse the child.

The aim of sexual grooming is to abuse or exploit in two ways:

1. Online sexual abuse. Children and young people being tricked or coerced into sexual activity over chat, video or photos.
2. A physical meeting. Persuading children and young people to meet them face to face in order to abuse them.

Grooming is also used by offenders with the aim of other forms of abuse, such as criminal exploitation or trafficking children. In all cases of grooming, it is never the child or young person's fault.

Signs of sexual grooming

Grooming works by using patterns of behaviours that allow an offender to make a child strongly believe that what is happening is ok, normal or love, or makes them feel trapped. Some of these behaviours are:

Building a relationship. Grooming is about making a child think that abuse and exploitation is normal, or that they have no choice. Offenders do this by building a relationship and emotional connection with the child.

What might be happening?

♦ trying to convince the child that they are in a loving relationship as boyfriend or girlfriend
♦ relationship building over a short space of time – not seeking to be a boyfriend or girlfriend, but to make a quick connection. May be through flattery or pretending to have lots in common
♦ becoming a mentor to the young person, making them think they are someone who can help them or teach them things
♦ becoming a dominant figure in a young person's life, perhaps by having a relationship with their parent or carer
♦ building a relationship with the child's family, making them think that they are someone who can be trusted with the child

Gaining power over a child. In all grooming, the offender will try to gain power over the child, to manipulate or coerce them.

What might be happening?

♦ emotionally intimidating the child by threatening to withdraw their affection or saying things like, 'if you loved me you would'
♦ telling the child there will be terrible consequences for refusing to do something sexual
♦ mimicking love. If a young person feels they are in love, this gives an offender power
♦ developing a dependency on drugs or alcohol so they can control them through addiction
♦ meeting a need, such as emotional needs, shelter, money

Keeping it secret. In all cases offenders will try to make sure that the child doesn't tell anyone else about the abuse.

What might be happening?

♦ telling the child that no one will believe them
♦ threatening to share secrets that the child has told them
♦ telling children that they have done something illegal and will be in trouble
♦ using the above power advantages against the child

What's different about grooming online?

Grooming happens in very similar ways in person and online, but can be easier for offenders to do online because:

♦ games, social media, live streaming platforms and chatrooms provide opportunities for them to make contact with children to try to groom them
♦ they can create multiple online identities and even pretend to be children and young people to trick real children into chatting and sharing
♦ they can find out a lot about children before they make contact by looking at the things the child has posted. Using this information they can target children and carefully plan what they will say and show an interest in
♦ they can also contact lots of children very quickly in the hope that one will respond

Remember

Many children and young people don't understand that they have been groomed, or that what has happened is abuse. Even if they tell you, or you find out about the abuse, young people may attempt to keep in contact with the offender and have very mixed feelings about it all. Talking with someone external, such as Childline, may help them. It's also important to let your child know that you are there for them, you know it isn't their fault and you are willing to support them.

Men have more relaxed attitudes to sexual abuse of boys by women like Emmerdale's Maya

Men find the sexual abuse of teenage boys by women less concerning than the abuse of teenage girls by men, research by Barnardo's shows.

The national children's charity has found that people overall have a more relaxed attitude to boys being groomed and abused by older women like in ITV's Emmerdale but that the most marked difference was among men.

In a survey conducted by YouGov*, Barnardo's found that more than a quarter (26%) of men who were presented with a variety of scenarios that have played out in the ITV soap said they would have found them more concerning if the perpetrator had been male and the teenage victim female.

Overall, one-in-five UK adults (20%) had this view and, of these, nearly two-thirds (64%) said it was because they think teenage girls are more vulnerable than teenage boys. More than a quarter (28%) thought it was every teenage boy's dream to be with an older woman.

Barnardo's has been advising Emmerdale on its abuse storyline which has seen schoolteacher Maya groom and abuse her pupil Jacob and has been praised for highlighting an important issue.

In last night's episode viewers were shocked when, after months of grooming him, Maya and Jacob had sex just a few days after his 16th birthday.

Barnardo's Chief Executive Javed Khan said: 'This research shows that even in 2019, many people don't recognise that sexual abuse of boys is just as serious as sexual abuse of girls.

'These outdated attitudes lead to boys missing out on vital support. They are much less likely than girls to be identified as victims of sexual abuse by professionals, who often don't see them as victims.

'In fact, boys can be groomed by older men or older women, exploiting feelings of loneliness, their need for care and their desire to be loved before abusing them, just like Maya has done with Jacob in Emmerdale.

'We need to get out of the "Mrs Robinson" mind-set. Abuse is abuse whether it happens to a boy or a girl or whether it's perpetrated by a man or a woman, and it can cause long term harm, affecting attitudes to love, relationships and sex in adulthood.'

Separate research conducted by Barnardo's last year and funded by the Home Office found that boys and young men often miss out on the support they would receive if they were girls because professionals don't always recognise them as victims.

It revealed that professionals may have difficulty in identifying and engaging boys and young men in terms of their history of abuse and trauma and that behaviour that might trigger concerns that girls are at risk is sometimes put down to 'boys being boys', leaving many victims without the specialist support they need.

The Children's Commissioner estimates that more than a quarter of child sexual abuse victims are boys and, according to the Department for Education's Children in Need census, more than a third of children on child protection plans for sexual abuse are boys.

Research from the Centre of Expertise on Child Sexual Abuse shows that 15% of girls and 5% of boys experience some form of sexual abuse before the age of 16.

The charity said that the introduction of compulsory relationships and sex education in English schools next year, which it long campaigned for, will help children and young people understand abuse and unhealthy or risky situations.

Javed Khan added: 'Addressing these topics in the classroom will help keep children safe and healthy, and prepare them for challenges on and offline.

'We know from our specialist work on child sexual abuse across the country how important it is to teach children and young people about consent, healthy relationships, how to spot the signs of abuse and how to ask for help.'

In its most recent research, Barnardo's polled more than 2,000 people and all respondents were asked whether they were willing to take part in the survey since it dealt with sensitive issues involving child sexual abuse.

Half were presented with a variety of abusive scenarios involving an older woman and a teenage boy exchanging text messages containing explicit images. The other half were presented with the same scenarios with the genders of the perpetrator and victim reversed.

In one sample, 17% of men thought that a woman in her 30s and a 16-year-old boy exchanging text messages containing explicit images was not concerning, compared to 2% of women. In the second sample, people were presented with the same scenario involving a 16-year-old girl and a man in his 30s instead of a woman and a boy. Only 7% of men said this was not concerning.

Likewise, one-in-10 men in the first sample thought that a female teacher and her 16 year old male student having sex was not concerning, compared to just 2% of women. When the genders of the perpetrator and victim were reversed for the second sample, only 4% of men were unconcerned.

Actress Louisa Clein who plays Maya told the Mirror: 'This story is fascinating because it's an older woman and a younger boy.

'We see it on social media – a lot of people are like get in there, lad, you've got yourself an older woman, a cougar. But it is still abuse, it is still sexual exploitation.

'If it was an older man to a younger girl or boy, immediately people would be saying that is wrong.'

To help Emmerdale tell the abuse storyline authentically, Barnardo's arranged for their researchers, story team and actors - including Louisa and Joe-Warren Plant who plays

Jacob - to meet experts and young men who have been supported by Barnardo's Better Futures project.

Louisa added: 'It is so damaging. These kids are 14, 15, 16 and they are at such a vulnerable age, so confused. He doesn't know what he is doing – he is 15 years old.

'He is in this social media world, sex is so accessible and he doesn't know the boundaries, and she's not showing the boundaries.'

In Emmerdale, Louisa's character Maya has used the following tactics to groom and abuse Jacob:

Targeting the victim

A groomer will identify a vulnerability within the intended victim. Children with limited support from trusted adults and/or less involved parents are more desirable, although all young people by their very nature are potential victims.

Gaining the victim's trust

The groomer gains their victim's trust by working out what the child's needs are and how to fill them. They may make the child feel understood and valued.

Filling a need

The groomer may then fill the void in the child's needs. They may provide drink, drugs, somewhere to stay, thoughtful gifts – but most significantly, the groomer will make the child feel loved and special.

Isolating the child

The groomer may encourage the child to sever protective contacts with family and friends and assume a protective and understanding position.

Sexualising the relationship

After the emotional attachment and trust of the child has been obtained, the groomer progressively sexualises the relationship. Desensitisation of the child may occur through talking, watching pornography and having sexual contact. The child may begin to see their relationship in more special terms.

Maintaining control

Once the sexual abuse has begun, child sex abusers use secrecy, blame and threats to manipulate the child into silence and participation. Threats may be made against the child's family and friends. The abuser may also threaten to circulate indecent/abusive images.

*All figures, unless otherwise stated, are from YouGov Plc. Total sample size was 2078 adults, of which 2,011 were willing to take part. Fieldwork was undertaken between 12th-13th February 2019. The survey was carried out online. The figures have been weighted and are representative of all UK adults (aged 18+). Half were presented with a variety of abusive scenarios involving an older woman and a teenage boy exchanging text messages containing explicit images. The other half were presented with the same scenarios with the genders of the perpetrator and victim reversed.

4 March 2019

New report details how sexual predators abused children in grassroots sport

Study by Independent Inquiry into Child Sexual Abuse and Truth Project explores experiences of nine victims between 1950s and early 2010s.

By Samuel Lovett

A new report into child sexual abuse in sport has detailed how coaches and instructors exploited children's vulnerabilities in order to groom and abuse them.

The study, published by the Independent Inquiry into Child Sexual Abuse and its Truth Project initiative, analyses the accounts of nine victims and survivors who played a wide range of sport, including football, boxing and gymnastics, between the 1950s and early 2010s.

It highlights how abuse was conducted at a grassroots level. For almost all the participants, sport was a hobby and, in the case of some, provided a distraction or diversion from a difficult home life.

Survivors spoke of being subjected to a wide range of sexually abusive behaviour, which was often perpetrated under the guise of a sporting activity.

'Say you'd be on any sort of residential trip, they'd be running in showers, taking pictures of the children naked, whilst they were having a shower. And it was all done out of like a laugh and joke,' one participant in the study told Truth Project.

The report also explores how grooming was used to build the trust of those being abused. Gifts and trips away were offered to victims, as were privileges or rewards within the sports club. At the same time, perpetrators sought to normalise certain actions, such as making sexualised comments or showing children pornographic material.

'As much as he was abusing me, he'd then put me in positions of power. So, I'd go to conferences, and he'd turn up and he was going to that conference. You know, always had me in his sights,' a survivor said.

These abuses were allowed to take place due to a lack of supervision and oversight of other coaches and leaders working in the relevant sports, the study found, highlighting in particular the danger of overnight trips with children.

The Offside Trust, which campaigns to keep children in sport safe, believes that predatory youth coaches in football exchanged grooming tactics and shared victims. Authorities were either oblivious to their actions or dismissed concerns raised against them.

Techniques used by Barry Bennell and Gordon Neely, two coaches who abused young footballers between the 1970s and 1990s, share similarities. Both paedophiles would terrorise the children with ghost stories and horror films before attempting to comfort them.

Victims who spoke to the Truth Project also highlighted the extensive impacts of the abuse on multiple areas of their lives, with many describing how decades later this still affects them on a daily basis.

Paul Stewart, a former professional footballer who played for Manchester City and Tottenham, said: 'Whilst the physical and sexual abuse I experienced as a child in a sports setting was horrendous, for me it was the impact it had in later life. It stripped me of everything – the ability to love and trust, and it also left me constantly thinking of a way out.'

Another survivor said: 'It's horrendous. You carry it with you forever. And it's like when I switched on and realised that it's the vulnerability of everything, you know. For the rest of your life you'll feel vulnerable.'

Dr Sophia King, a principal researcher at the Independent Inquiry into Child Sexual Abuse, said it was 'clear' that the inability to disclose these experiences, as well as the fear of not being believed, acted as a significant obstacle to children reporting their abuse.

'In this report, victims and survivors describe how perpetrators in sports contexts would create opportunities for abuse, which often took place under the guise of sporting activity,' Dr King said.

'Participants' accounts were examined to provide a more in-depth insight into abuse in these contexts, with many reporting that they were groomed as a way to normalise what was happening.'

Mr Stewart added: 'It's important that survivors have the opportunity to come forward if they wish to do so, and the Truth Project provides that place to share an experience, free from judgement.

'I hope this report can help to contribute to a more open conversation about abuse in sport at all levels, and shines a light on experiences like mine. We need to ensure the words that survivors have shared with the Truth Project are learnt from, and listened to.'

The Independent Inquiry is examining the extent to which institutions and organisations have failed to protect children in England and Wales from sexual abuse. Its Truth Project programme has heard from more than 4,800 victims and survivors.

18 June 2020

Rise in child abuse online threatens to overwhelm UK police, officers warn

Sheer quantity of abusive material hindering detection while Facebook move to greater encryption is a further blow.

By Harriet Grant

The vast, and growing, volume of child abuse material being created and shared online is threatening to overwhelm police efforts to tackle it, senior officers have told the Guardian.

And the situation is likely to worsen, National Crime Agency (NCA) child abuse lead Rob Jones warned, if social media sites such as Facebook press ahead with further encryption of messaging services.

Law enforcement against online child abuse in the UK was 'the best in the world by some distance', Jones said. 'But we are arresting and dealing with more offenders than ever, the numbers are growing and growing, as are the number of children being safeguarded.'

The numbers involved are staggering. The UK's child abuse image database has 17 million unique images on it, and it is growing by 500,000 every two months.

Children were posting pictures of themselves online and predators were targeting them, Jones explained.

'Children sharing videos and photos online has exploded,' he said. 'And once a child posts an image it can become a honey pot for offenders posing as children. They link and chat to the child and it is very, very quick that the child is compromised. Often they are too scared to reach out for help.'

Simon Bailey, the National Police Chiefs' Council lead for child protection, described the horror of this abuse, which mainly targets girls aged between 11 and 13.

'You see a young person who is being told to insert objects inside themselves, and in the background you hear mum calling them down for their dinner.'

Once images of the child have been sent to an abuser, 'they are out in the wild, recirculating,' Jones warned.

'They are told to abuse a child to gain entry'

One of the key messages Jones wants to get across is that when abusive images are shared it is not on the dark web, but on open, easy-to-access sites.

'Child abuse is three or four clicks away,' he said. 'There is no block, no barrier to entry at all. Any search engine will allow people with a sexual interest in children to meet like-minded individuals who normalise it, rationalise it, encourage it. They will then move to closed chat forums where they will be told they need to abuse a child to gain entry to image-sharing sites.'

All of this, he said, was exacerbated by children's increasing dependence on the online world.

'[The lockdown] has seen children completely relying on the internet to live their lives,' he pointed out. 'And keeping pace with that dependence is difficult for parents.'

A key part of the work the NCA does is to stop children being 'revictimised' as their images are shared again and again by paedophiles. One way this is done is using photo hashes, digital files that match known images of child abuse and are used to scan sites such as Facebook, Google or the game platform Roblox.

Facebook has said it plans to encrypt its Messenger service, bringing it in line with WhatsApp and Instagram, which it also owns.

'If encryption goes ahead we stand to lose it all,' Jones said. 'As companies move to end-to-end encryption there is a real risk that all the leads we talk about, the monitoring of known images that often lead us directly to offenders, will be lost.

'More and more children are being groomed and abused and it's not as if the industry doesn't know this. They are fully informed and have chosen to ignore the horrors of what we find daily.'

Last month, Facebook told British MPs that encryption would mean scanning technologies would no longer pick up as much child abuse material.

Monika Bickert, the firm's head of global policy management, told the home affairs select committee that the company would not be able to pass on as many reports of child abuse. 'I would expect the numbers to go down. If content is being shared and … it's content we cannot see then it's content we cannot report,' she said.

Responding to the criticism from the NCA, a spokesperson for Facebook insisted that they would still be tackling abuse on their platforms:

'Facebook has led the industry in developing new ways to prevent, detect, and respond to abuse. End-to-end encryption is already the leading technology used by many services to keep people safe online and, when we roll it out on our other messaging services, we will build on our strong anti-abuse capabilities at WhatsApp. For example, WhatsApp bans around 250,000 accounts each month suspected of sharing child exploitative imagery.'

Between April and September last year, 4,700 people, nearly all men, were arrested for online child abuse offences and more than 6,000 children were safeguarded.

Jones is particularly concerned over the growth of live streaming, where paedophiles pay to watch children abused in poorer countries.

'Live streaming is a marker for severe offending,' he said. 'That is what is terrifying about this casework. Offenders have become so desensitised that to receive sexual gratification they will ask for very specific, bespoke abuse to be carried out.'

'My great fear,' Jones added, 'is that with increasing access to technology around the world, more children and poor families who can't afford to feed their children will be exposed to this risk.'

Because live streaming is difficult to track in real time it was vital, Bailey and Jones said, to protect access to messaging services where images will be shared.

'This is the low-hanging fruit,' Jones said. 'The monitoring of known images can often lead us directly to offenders. The technology is there to prevent it, but the internet companies are not doing enough to tackle the threat.'

9 February 2021

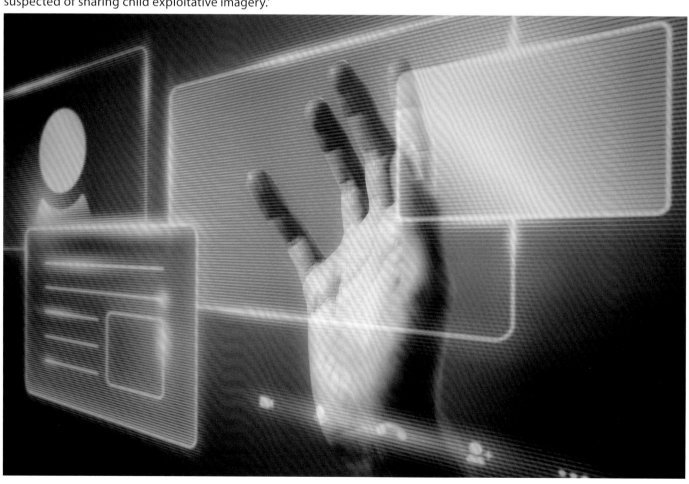

Child abuse cases in Scotland soar as sex offence figures rise by a third

Police Scotland data requested by children's charity NSPCC show there were 5311 recorded offences in 2019-20.

By Daniel Harkins

Sexual offences against children in Scotland have risen by almost a third in the past five years, figures show.

Police Scotland data requested by children's charity NSPCC show there were 5311 recorded offences in 2019-20 – an average of 15 a day and up 30 per cent in the five years since 2014-15.

This include incidents of rape, online grooming and sexual assault.

The most recent figures show girls were five times as likely to be victims.

A total of 1588 offences were against children under 13, about 45 per cent of crimes where age was recorded.

NSPCC Scotland's Matt Forde said: 'Every day, children in Scotland are being sexually abused and having to live with the devastating impacts of this. Urgent action is needed to prevent abuse and ensure children are supported to recover when it is disclosed.

'We have seen numerous plans and initiatives launched to deal with various aspects of abuse, including child sexual exploitation and harmful sexual behaviour.

'We believe it's crucial to have a joined-up approach when tackling this crime and want to see a strategy which puts the experiences and needs of children at its heart.'

NSPCC Scotland has called on the Scottish Government to produce a strategy to combat child sexual abuse. It said the availability of specialist therapeutic sexual abuse services is 'patchy and inconsistent'.

It believes health, policing, social work, therapeutic and other services should be provided to children in one location.

The Scottish Government said: 'Child sexual abuse requires a co-ordinated, multi-agency response and we are revising Scotland's National Child Protection Guidance.'

10 August 2020

Many children have been the victims of grooming gangs, but there's no evidence for a figure of one million

By Leo Benedictus

What was claimed

A million children have been gang raped and groomed in the UK.

Our verdict

This figure is not reliable. It appears to come from assuming that the number of suspected cases of child sexual exploitation in 2018/19 can be multiplied by 30 years—which still does not reach one million. We don't know what the true number is.

A widely shared post on Facebook compares the public reaction to the killing of George Floyd with the reaction to the organised sexual abuse of children in the UK.

It says: 'The cops kill a man in America, massive civil unrest. 1 million innocent children gang raped & groomed in the UK. Nothing happens.'

It is difficult to compare the reaction to the killing of George Floyd in the US with the reaction to cases of child sexual exploitation in the UK. Comparing the seriousness of the two issues and the adequacy of the public and official responses would involve complex and subjective judgements.

However, we can consider the claim that one million children have been gang raped and groomed in the UK. It isn't clear what period of time the figure is meant to cover, or exactly what type of abuse it is describing, but if it refers to the victims of grooming gangs in particular, we cannot find evidence to support it.

How many children are abused?

According to the most recent Crime Survey for England and Wales (CSEW), 7.5% of adults aged 18 to 74 years experienced sexual abuse before they were 16. This would make a total of 3.1 million children within living memory, and more if we include Scotland and Northern Ireland, and people who are now older than 74.

This post, however, mentions children 'gang raped and groomed', and comes from a Facebook account called 'South Yorkshire Grooming Gangs Awareness'. It appears to be connected with Rotherham, a town where more than 1,400 children were abused by a gang over a number of years. There have been many similar cases elsewhere. We think therefore that it refers specifically to the number of victims of child sexual exploitation by grooming gangs, but the post is unclear.

When asked in the comments below the post for a source of the '1 million figure', the author replied, '19,000 girls a year for 30 years, you do the maths', and added a link to an article in the *Independent* from 2019.

The article reported that 18,700 children had been identified as suspected victims of child sexual exploitation in 2018/19, according to Department for Education figures that the Independent had seen.

This did not describe victims of grooming gangs in particular. These are also not confirmed cases, nor does the number account for any other cases that were not identified. We also can't assume that the same number of children had been sexually exploited each year for the past 30 years, as the Facebook post does. (If it were the case that there were 19,000 victims a year over 30 years, this would make a total of 570,000.)

Another one million claim

In an interview about the Rotherham case in 2015 the MP for Rotherham, Sarah Champion, also said: 'There are hundreds of thousands and I think there could be up to a million victims of exploitation nationwide, including right now.'

When we asked Ms Champion where this figure came from, she told us that she had calculated it herself as a rough estimate. 'I extrapolated that Rotherham is a town [of] 200,000 and had 1,400 known victims of CSE [child sexual exploitation] between 1997-2013 and 15% of women report their rape - so scaled up,' she said.

This is not a reliable way to calculate an estimate either. We do not know whether Rotherham's experience is typical of the whole country. Also, we think the 15% figure Ms Champion used comes from a government report from 2013. If so, it represents the proportion of women who reported the most recent incident of serious sexual assault they had experienced, which is not necessarily the same as the proportion of child exploitation victims indentified in Rotherham.

It might be possible to create an estimate of one million victims by speculating about cases that happened decades ago, but in the recent past it does not seem likely that one million children have been the victims of child grooming gangs, or sexual exploitation more widely. Even so, it is a serious problem on a large scale.

Further information and confidential advice about child abuse can be found via the Child Exploitation and Online Protection Centre and the Lucy Faithfull Foundation's Stop It Now! service.

We've rated this claim as false because there appears to be no evidence to support the figure of one million.

24 July 2020

Child sex abuse survivors are five times more likely to be the victims of sexual assault later in life

An article from *The Conversation*.

THE CONVERSATION

By Nina Papalia, Postdoctoral Research Fellow, Centre for Forensic Behavioural Science, Victorian Institute of Forensic Mental Health (Forensicare), Swinburne University of Technology & James Oglof, University Distinguished Professor of Forensic Behavioural Science, Director of the Centre for Forensic Behavioural Science, Swinburne University of Technology

As Australia's landmark Royal Commission into Institutional Responses to Child Sexual Abuse and other cases have shown, the impact of child sexual abuse is devastating.

Adverse mental health outcomes are the most recognised and researched effects of abuse. These can include post-traumatic stress disorder, depression, anxiety and feelings of guilt, shame, anger and low self-esteem.

Re-victimisation, or the likelihood that child sexual abuse survivors will experience further sexual abuse later in life, is a particularly tragic consequence that is rarely mentioned or considered.

To prevent this cycle of victimisation, we must understand the scope of the links between child sex abuse and re-victimisation later in life, why it exists and which survivors are most vulnerable. Our research aimed to answer some of these questions.

What we already know and what our research did

Previous studies have confirmed a strong relationship between child sexual abuse and adult sexual re-victimisation. A 2017 review of research on these links found that about half of child survivors have been sexually victimised later in life.

Previous studies, however, have been limited since they typically:

◆ ask adults to recall their experiences of child sexual abuse, which many find difficult to remember accurately or to disclose

◆ have asked people to recall experiences of both abuse and re-victimisation at the same time, which doesn't provide a picture of these relationships over time

◆ consider only female survivors, meaning we know little about re-victimisation in men who have been abused as children

◆ do not explore factors that make re-victimisation more or less likely to occur.

We attempted to remedy these limitations in our research by re-analysing data of 2,759 Australian boys and girls who were medically confirmed to have been sexually abused between 1964 and 1995. The files were drawn from children examined by independent medical practitioners from the Victorian Institute of Forensic Medicine as part of legal investigations.

To determine whether they had been re-victimised later in life, we then traced their contacts with police as victims of crimes as adults (to an average age of 35) – and considered the lifetime frequency and types of crimes they were victims of.

We compared these findings to a sample from the general population not known to have been sexually abused in childhood. This is what we found:

Re-victimisation is not limited to sexual offences or just women

Overall, most (64%) child sexual abuse survivors in our study were not re-victimised later in life. This percentage was consistent with the control group (67% were not victims of crimes).

Unfortunately, though, child sexual abuse survivors were much more likely than those in the control group to be re-victimised in what are considered medium and high harm personal injury crimes.

For instance, they were five times more likely to have been victims of sexual assault later in life, twice as likely to be victims of physical assault, four times as likely to be threatened with violence and twice as likely to be stalked.

We also found the increased risk of re-victimisation was not just experienced by women. For example, male survivors of child sex abuse were seven times more likely to be the victims of a further sexual assault than the men in the control group.

Why child sex abuse survivors are more vulnerable

The reasons why child sexual abuse is linked to re-victimisation are not well known. Nor are the factors that determine which survivors are more vulnerable to crimes later in life.

Prevailing theories suggest re-victimisation is not the result of any one factor. Rather, it is the combination of different factors in survivors' lives – some having to do with personal characteristics and experiences, others having to do with their environments.

We investigated the role of certain personal factors in whether child sex survivors were re-victimised later in life.

Specifically, we studied the impact of three things: gender, the characteristics of the child sex abuse (such as the age when it occurred, type, frequency), and different types of mental illness. Three overall patterns emerged:

First, female survivors were more likely than male survivors to experience sexual re-victimisation. In contrast, male survivors were at greater risk for being the victims of non-sexual violent crimes and non-violent crimes, such as property crimes.

Second, the age when child sexual abuse occurred played a significant role in predicting later re-victimisation. Survivors who were younger than 12 when they were abused were more likely to be the victims of both sexual and violent crimes later in life.

Third, and perhaps most concerning, child sex abuse survivors who developed mental illness were more vulnerable to re-victimisation.

How mental illness factors into re-victimisation

The links between mental illness and re-victimisation, however, were complex.

Child sex abuse survivors who developed personality disorders or anxiety disorders, for example, were roughly twice as likely to be victims of all types of crimes as adults compared to survivors who did not develop these conditions.

Other mental illnesses were linked to some forms of re-victimisation, but not others. Post-traumatic stress disorders, for example, were linked with higher rates of sexual re-victimisation. Mood disorders were linked to violent re-victimisation.

And survivors who developed substance abuse issues were more likely to become victims of both violent and non-violent crimes later in life.

There are at least two explanations for these links.

First, symptoms of mental illness may impair a survivor's capacity to recognise and respond to risky situations and people. Offenders are also more likely to target child sex abuse survivors because of their vulnerability.

Second, survivors who suffer re-victimisation later in life may be more prone to serious mental health problems due to the cumulative impacts of repeat abuse. That is, mental illness may be a consequence of, not a contributor to, this continuous cycle of abuse.

The truth is that both explanations likely contribute to the relationship between mental illness and re-victimisation.

Meeting the needs of survivors

It is difficult to establish a direct causal link between child sexual abuse and re-victimisation over one's lifespan. But it's clear that for some survivors, victimisation is an ongoing problem rather than just an isolated event.

Victoria's Royal Commission into the Mental Health System has highlighted the barriers trauma survivors experience in accessing appropriate support services. The strong links we found between mental illness and re-victimisation support further integration of mental health and victim services.

More research into why child sexual abuse is linked with re-victimisation – and which survivors are most at risk – may help to better focus prevention and treatment efforts.

A final word about resilience

Despite the odds, most abuse survivors are not re-victimised later in life, according to our study. However, we understand that many people who are victims of child sex abuse – likely including some in our control group – do not report these crimes. As such, our estimates of re-victimisation are doubtless conservative.

We mustn't lose sight of the strength and resilience shown by survivors in the face of adversity. Understanding how this process of resilience occurs may provide useful insights about how to support other survivors to lead positive and fulfilling lives – without being re-victimised.

22 July 2020

Abused or neglected children are four times more likely to develop serious mental illness, study finds

A study by the University of Birmingham has shown that children who have experienced child abuse or neglect are four times more likely to develop serious mental illness such as psychoses, schizophrenia and bipolar disorder.

Researchers studied GP records dating between 1995 and 2018 of 217,758 patients aged under 18 who had experienced, or were suspected to have experienced, childhood maltreatment or related concerns, and then compared them to the records of 423,410 patients who had not.

The study, published today in *The Lancet Psychiatry*, found those patients who were maltreated were more than twice as likely to develop serious mental ill health such as psychoses, schizophrenia and bipolar disorder, or require a prescription to treat mental ill health, compared to those who have no recorded experience of maltreatment. The researchers also found maltreated children were more than twice as likely to develop some form of mental illness, such as depression or anxiety.

Childhood maltreatment, defined as any form of physical, sexual or emotional abuse and neglect, is a global public health and human rights issue affecting more than one in three children aged under 18 (i).

This was the biggest study of its kind to explore the association between abuse or neglect in childhood and the development of mental illness.

The researchers also found a clear under-recording of child maltreatment in GP records, and say potential opportunities to spot child maltreatment or implement management plans for these vulnerable individuals are being missed.

First author Dr Joht Singh Chandan, Academic Clinical Fellow in Public Health at the University of Birmingham's Institute of Applied Health Research, said: 'Our findings, along with evidence from other global studies, demonstrates the substantial burden of mental ill health following child abuse or neglect.

'Considering the prevalence of maltreatment, it is clear we are not doing enough to prevent and detect this important risk factor for mental ill health.

'There is a desperate need to rethink our public health approach to preventing and detecting childhood maltreatment and its associated negative consequences.'

Corresponding author Julie Taylor, Professor of Child Protection at the University of Birmingham's School of Nursing, said: 'Services aiming to build resilience in survivors of maltreatment have shown great promise in the reduction in the development of mental ill health.

'Our study, the first of this size and magnitude to have been conducted in the UK, emphasises the importance of early intervention in abused or neglected children's lives to prevent adverse outcomes.'

Corresponding author Dr Krish Nirantharakumar, also of the University of Birmingham, added: 'There is an important public health message to focus, not only on approaches that prevent or detect childhood maltreatment, but also to explore methods of prevention and detection of mental ill health in those who have experienced childhood maltreatment.

'Building resilience in children, families, local services and communities of those at risk might be a way of improving mental health outcomes.'

26 September 2019

Notes to Editors:
The University of Birmingham is ranked amongst the world's top 100 institutions. Its work brings people from across the world to Birmingham, including researchers, teachers and more than 6,500 international students from over 150 countries.
Chandan et al (2019). 'The burden of mental ill health associated with childhood maltreatment in the United Kingdom: A retrospective cohort study using The Health Improvement Network database'. Lancet Psychiatry. DOI: 10.1016/S2215-0366(19)30369-4
(i) World Health Organization. Violence Info – Child maltreatment. 2017. http://apps.who.int/violence-info/child-maltreatment/
This research was carried out by Dr Joht Singh Chandan, Dr Tom Thomas, Mr Krishna Margadhamane Gokhale, Professor Siddhartha Bandyopadhyay, Dr Krishnarajah Nirantharakumar and Professor Julie Taylor, all of the University of Birmingham.

Inquiry poll confirms 81% of child sexual abuse survivors feel stereotyped

New statistics from the Independent Inquiry into Child Sexual Abuse have found over three quarters of victims and survivors believe they were stereotyped after speaking out about their abuse.

Based on a poll of 116 survivors from the Inquiry's Victims and Survivors Forum, the findings revealed that more than half did not report the abuse because of concerns over how they would be seen by those around them. The Forum gives survivors of child sexual abuse the opportunity to meet, discuss and contribute to the Inquiry's work.

♦ 95 percent said that encouraging a more open conversation about child sexual abuse would help stop the stereotyping of victims and survivors

♦ 81 percent said they have felt stereotyped as a victim and survivor of child sexual abuse

♦ 69 percent said they did not speak out about the abuse due to fears of being stereotyped

'I do not trust anybody with the knowledge that I was abused as a child. I feel that people would look at me differently, either with pity or distrust that there must be something wrong with me now.'

Many survivors talked about how they felt 'put in a box' after disclosing their abuse, describing how they'd been labelled as emotionally unstable, damaged or weak. They explained the detrimental impact this had had on both their professional and personal lives.

'When I have disclosed my status as a survivor of child sexual abuse, I feel that people see me only as a victim. I have a senior role in business and people's attitudes towards me have definitely changed when I have told them. They see me as weak.'

One of the most common stereotypes mentioned was that those who were sexually abused as children would become abusers themselves.

Survivors described how assumptions contribute to the 'stigma and shame' which can still surround those impacted by child sexual abuse. They explained how stereotypes have acted as a barrier to them speaking out, or have prevented them from disclosing the abuse altogether.

'There have been too many obstacles to speaking out about my childhood experiences. Being stereotyped is just another one.'

The poll highlights the urgent need for society to break down the wall of silence around child sexual abuse in order to help improve understanding, awareness and the true impact that abuse can have on the lives of those affected.

'It is important for people to understand that the legacy of child abuse affects every aspect of a survivor's life. It has shaped our experience of the world and how we live moment to moment in it.'

95 percent of victims and survivors said that by encouraging a more open conversation, we can help stop the stereotyping of victims and survivors and ensure that those who feel ready to speak out are able to do so.

The Inquiry is calling for survivors to come forward to its Truth Project - over 4,000 people have now shared their experiences and made recommendations for change.

Inquiry Panel member Drusilla Sharpling said:

'Survivors of child sexual abuse come from all walks of life. If we are to make recommendations to keep children safe in future, we need to understand the wide range of survivor experiences.

'Whoever you are, and whatever your background, the Truth Project is here to listen to you.'

Survivors of child sexual abuse who would like to share their experiences in writing, over the phone or in person can get in touch with the Inquiry's Truth Project.

Visit www.truthproject.org.uk or email share@iicsa.org.uk

16 September 2019

Victims and Survivors Forum
Stereotypes and assumptions

95%
said that encouraging more open conversations about child sexual abuse would help stop the stereotyping of victims and survivors

The percentage of respondents who said that they have felt stereotyped as a victim and survivor of child sexual abuse

81%

"I feel that people only see me as a victim. I have a senior role in business and people's attitudes towards me have definately changed when I have told them"

Source: Independent Inquiry Child Sexual Abuse

Fathers' adverse childhood experiences are linked to their children's development

Correlations have been found between adverse childhood experiences in fathers' lives and sleep disruption, inattention, anger, and anxiety in their children.

By Duncan Fisher

New research from Romania has demonstrated a clear correlation between adverse childhood experiences in fathers' lives and their children's development, including sleep disruption, inattention, anger, and anxiety. Fathers' symptoms of depression partially accounted for the correlation between their early experiences and their children's inattention and anger. Fathers' negative parenting practices partially accounted for the link with children's inattention.

Adverse childhood experiences include growing up in poverty; absence or death of a parent; violence; caregivers' drug or alcohol addiction; physical or emotional neglect; peer victimization; or physical, psychological, and sexual abuse.

Based on the study, the researchers concluded that fathers should be involved in programs that support children with problems such as anxiety, anger, inattention, and sleep disturbance. Other studies have shown that parents with a reported history of prior maltreatment have the capacity for improving their parenting practices. Fathers should also receive direct support to address depression and negative parenting practices.

The study featured 118 fathers of 6- to 17-year-olds. All fathers were in stable, committed relationships with the mother of their children. Fathers completed a series of psychological questionnaires and evaluations of their own children. They were asked about their own childhood experiences, their assessment of their children's mental health (inattention, sleep disturbance, depression, anger, anxiety), their own parenting practices, and their relationship with their children's mother.

The correlations in this research do not imply causation, but they do correspond with earlier research, particularly on mothers. Mothers' depression and negative parenting has been shown to explain the link between their own adverse childhood experiences and their children's development – including communication, problem solving, motor skills at age 2, health, and hyperactivity. Many studies have confirmed that individuals who were maltreated in childhood are at risk of repeating these negative behaviours toward their own children.

Fathers' symptoms of depression have also been linked to their children's anxiety, depression, substance addiction (for up to 20 years), psychiatric disorders, lower academic performance, hyperactivity, social problems, and emotional difficulties. The global socioeconomic changes that have been occurring for the last 40 years suggest that the traditional mother-focused models of developmental influence are old fashioned. The presence and involvement of fathers in their children's lives is strongly associated with their offspring's social well-being, academic achievement, and behavioural adjustment. Moreover, longitudinal studies have confirmed that, in child development, fathers matter in ways similar to mothers.

January 2021

References
Seteanu SL & Giosan C (2020), Adverse childhood experiences in fathers and the consequences in their children, Professional Psychology: Research and Practice

Non-recent abuse

If you were abused in childhood, you may be struggling with difficult feelings and unwanted memories. We've got information and advice to help.

What is non-recent abuse?

Non-recent child abuse, sometimes called historical abuse, is when an adult was abused as a child or young person under the age of 18. Sometimes adults who were abused in childhood blame themselves or are made to feel it's their fault. But this is never the case: there's no excuse for abuse.

You might have known you were abused for a very long time or only recently learnt or understood what happened to you. Whether the abuse happened once or hundreds of times, a year or 70 years ago, whatever the circumstances, there's support to help you. It's never too late.

Effects of non-recent abuse

The impact of child abuse can last a lifetime. Abuse can have a huge effect on your health, relationships and education and can stop you from having the childhood and life you deserve. You might find it harder to cope with life's stresses, getting a job or being the type of parent you want to be. You may also develop mental health problems and drug or alcohol issues.

The effects can be short term but sometimes they last into adulthood. If someone has been abused as a child, it's more likely that they'll suffer abuse again. This is known as revictimisation.

The long term effects of abuse and neglect can include:

♦ emotional difficulties like anger, anxiety, sadness or low self-esteem

♦ mental health problems like depression, eating disorders, self harm or suicidal thoughts

♦ problems with drugs or alcohol

♦ disturbing thoughts, emotions and memories

♦ poor physical health

♦ struggling with parenting or relationships.

Support

If you were abused as a child, you deserve to be believed and get support if you want to. Whether you're speaking about the abuse for the first time or have had help in the past but need support again, there are people who can help.

Speak to a friend or family member

Thinking about talking to someone close to you about the abuse can seem frightening. You might not know where to start or may be worried about their reaction. It's important to choose someone you feel you can trust to provide a listening ear.

You don't have to tell them everything. Even if you say very little, speaking to them might help to lighten the load and help you think about what you want to do next.

NAPAC is the National Association for People Abused in Childhood. NAPAC's trained staff speak with survivors of any type of childhood abuse over the phone, exploring the options available to them such as support groups and counselling to help empower callers to move forward. Calls

'It took me a long time to understand what happened to me as a child and the impact it's had. But speaking to family, friends, my partner and NAPAC helped me get the support I needed.' – Rupa / NSPCC staff

are confidential, free from UK landlines and mobiles and can me made anonymously.

NAPAC also supports family members, friends and professionals who are helping someone who was abused, advising them on who else can help.

The NAPAC website provides a wealth of information and advice, including a postcode searchable database which lists local trusted organisations who can offer free or low-cost on-going support.

Talk to your GP about seeing a counsellor

Talking to your GP might be helpful. They can refer you on to appropriate support, like counselling, and let you know if the NHS has services for survivors in your local area.

You can also search for a private counsellor using the British Association for Counselling and Psychotherapy website.

Finding the right counsellor for you can take time. If therapy hasn't helped you in the past, it might be better for you to try a different counsellor. Ask them whether they have experience of supporting adults who were abused in childhood.

Reporting non-recent abuse

It's never too late to report abuse you experienced. But you don't have to report it to anyone if you don't want to. And no one should pressure or force you to do anything you don't want to.

Some people report non-recent abuse to stop the offender abusing other children. Some find that reporting gives them a sense of closure and helps them to start moving on.

If you do decide to, you can speak to the police about what happened to you. You can report abuse to the police no matter how long ago it happened. You can start by calling 101 and briefly explaining what you're calling about. They'll make sure you're put through to the right team who can support you.

It's normal to be anxious about reporting and worry about what might happen. If you don't feel comfortable contacting the police or want to find out more about your options, you can contact us. We're here to support you, no matter your worry. Call us on 0808 800 5000, visit our website nspcc.org. uk or email help@nspcc.org.uk

Alice's story

Alice had a rough childhood. The abuse happened when she was six and again at 16. She still has flashbacks. But she's moving on now. She's signed to a record label. She's meeting people and doing what she loves.

A part of life

Alice was six when she was sexually abused by her father. 'I didn't have a clue at the time what had happened; I just knew I was upset and something was wrong.'

She grew up thinking abuse was a part of childhood. When she was drugged and abused at a house party, she thought it was normal. 'I thought I was on the planet just to be used by men'.

Alice became a very anxious 16 year old. Every time she left the house, she would face her abusers. She started missing school and stopped going out with mates.

As much as she wanted to, Alice couldn't talk to her mum about it. 'I was a carer for her and she has bipolar, so it was very hard to talk to her.' Alice toughed it out alone, unsure what her future would look like, until she met Suzanne.

Picking up the pieces

Suzanne is one of our practitioners who specialises in child sexual abuse and exploitation. She was a stable presence in Alice's life, someone Alice could depend on.

'I know I can talk to her about anything. I was able to ring her even when we weren't in sessions.'

Together they worked through the signs and dangers of sexual exploitation. Alice began to make sense of what had happened. She now knows if someone is trying to take advantage and has the confidence to get out of dangerous situations. 'I've been able to put it all into action'.

'I've been able to pick myself up.'

Since meeting Suzanne, Alice has become more confident and no longer self harms.

'My self worth is now there.'

She still gets anxiety and painful flashbacks, but she is determined to challenge them. Alice no longer sees herself as someone to be abused.

'I am more than that.'

Making music

Today, Alice is a signed musician. She's always loved singing but now she's doing it for real.

'I've come a long way.'

It will get better...

...you will survive this

She's also the person people talk to when they've got something going on. 'I can always take at least one positive out of all the negative things'.

She likes it when people call on her. 'It always makes me feel better, because I want to go into helping people.'

'I'm more positive about the future.'

Alice still feels anxious and scared at times, but she doesn't let it drag her down. She is optimistic about her future and wants to give something back.

'If there's one message that I could give to other young people, who are having their own challenges, it would be there's always a way to get out of a bad situation. There is always a way, no matter how deep you're into something.'

This is a true story but names and identifying details have been changed to protect the young person.

Sex abuse 'loophole' to be closed with law to ban sports coaches and priests taking advantage of under 18s

The move comes after a number of revelations involving sports coaches taking advantage of young people in their care.

By Benjamin Butterworth, Late Editor and Senior Reporter

Sports coaches and religious leaders who have sex with 16- and 17-year olds in their care are to face prosecution under proposals to protect children from abuse.

The Positions of Trust Law will prevent adults in a position of authority and with direct contact from engaging in sexual relationships with people under 18.

Thousands of advocates, including MPs and charities, backed the campaign to close the 'loophole' in the Sexual Offences Act, which already applies to roles such as teachers and social workers.

The move comes after a four-year campaign by children's charity NSPCC following a number of cases involving sports coaches taking advantage of people in their care.

Peter Wanless, NSPCC chief executive, said: 'We are delighted that after relentless campaigning, the Government has finally listened to our calls and agreed to close this legal loophole.

'This landmark step sends a clear message that children and young people can return to the extracurricular activities they love without being at risk of grooming by the very adults they should look to for support and guidance.'

Campaigners are also calling for professions such as driving instructors, still not covered by the proposals, to be added to the list.

Justice Secretary Robert Buckland said there will be power in the Bill to 'include other categories in future'.

A Ministry of Justice spokesman said: 'The move follows an extensive review which raised concerns that predators could exploit the particular influence these roles can often have in a young person's life – making them vulnerable to abuse.'

9 March 2021

Scotland becomes first UK nation to ban smacking of children

Law comes into force giving same protection from assault as adults.

Scotland has become the first part of the UK to ban the smacking of children after new legislation came into effect.

Changes to the law giving children the same protection from assault as adults were passed by the Scottish parliament last year and take effect from Saturday.

Scotland becomes the 58th country to outlaw corporal punishment after the defence of justifiable assault was removed from Scots law.

It is the first part of the UK to do so, with Wales expected to follow suit with the introduction of a ban by 2022.

The Scottish Green MSP John Finnie, who introduced the changes, said he hoped the smacking ban would help demonstrate to children that violence is not acceptable.

He said: 'As I have progressed my campaign over the last four years, it has been noticeable just how many people believed that striking a child was already outlawed.

'I am pleased that this will now be the case.'

The children's minister, Maree Todd, said: 'I'm very pleased that Scotland has become the first part of the UK to legislate to ensure that children, without exception, have the same protection from assault as adults.

'This outdated defence has no place in a modern Scotland. It can never be reasonable to strike a child.'

Joanna Barrett, the NSPCC Scotland policy and public affairs officer, said: 'This new law, finally, gives children in Scotland their rightful protection against assault and the same safeguards as adults.

'By making this common-sense move to get rid of the outdated defence of "justifiable assault", we will be joining more than 50 other countries around the world in taking measures to protect the most vulnerable members of society.

'This law sets out in clear terms that physical punishment should no longer be part of childhood in Scotland and it marks a momentous step in making it a country where children's rights are truly recognised, respected and fulfilled.'

The Liberal Democrat MSP Alex Cole-Hamilton said he was 'delighted' about the change to the law.

He said: 'The abolition of this Victorian-sounding legal defence is long overdue.

'It is backed by countless studies and experts from the children's commissioner to police officers, social workers, nurses, and children's and parenting charities.

'It sends a clear message about what kind of country we aspire to be. After defying the UN for years on this, the Scottish government now need to stop ignoring other international human rights minimums such as setting the age of criminal responsibility at 14.'

But campaign group Be Reasonable Scotland, which opposed the legislation, warned that 'even the mildest physical discipline will be treated as abuse' and could lead to parents being prosecuted.

A spokesman for the group said: 'In the years ahead, loving parents who have had no contact with the authorities previously and who present no risk to their children will face stressful intervention, blacklisting on police databases and even criminal records for smacking.

'The majority of Scots see this as an injustice, not a positive change.'

7 November 2020

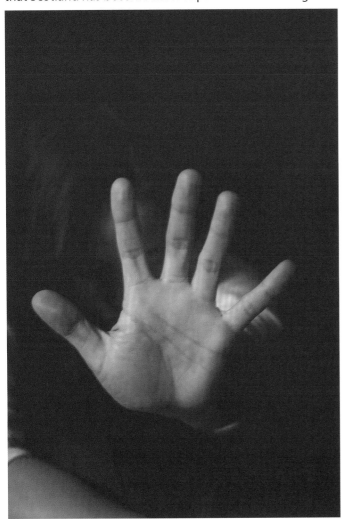

Facebook encryption will create 'hidden space' for paedophiles to abuse children, National Crime Agency warns

Warning issued as predator who targeted thousands of children on Facebook Messenger jailed.

By Lizzie Dearden, Home Affairs Correspondent

Facebook's encryption plans will create a 'hidden space' where paedophiles can abuse children beyond the reach of law enforcement, the National Crime Agency (NCA) has warned.

Senior officials said the UK received 12 million tips over child sex abuse images and suspicious activity from the social network last year, and that if the 'taps get turned off' fewer offenders will be arrested and more children could be at risk.

The NCA's warning came as one of the UK's most prolific paedophiles, David Wilson, was jailed for using Facebook to target up to 5,000 children while posing as a teenage girl.

In March 2019, Mark Zuckerberg announced that Facebook was working towards end-to-end encryption on all its messaging services that would 'prevent anyone – including us – from seeing what people share'.

Rob Jones, the NCA's director for threat leadership, said Facebook's plans would risk 'abuse spiralling out of control in a hidden space that is created'.

'It poses an existential threat to child protection,' he told a press conference.

'It creates a private space where people like Wilson can masquerade as children, engage with children, groom them and develop either coercive control and make them abuse themselves and send images to them, or meet them in the real world and abuse them themselves.'

Wilson posed as a teenage girl on numerous fake Facebook accounts to dupe boys as young as four into sending him sexual images.

The Norfolk roofer, who lived with his mother, contacted up to 5,000 children globally and was sent content by around 500 victims. Several were then blackmailed into sending more extreme footage, and forced to abuse younger siblings or friends.

Priti Patel called the case 'a chilling reminder of how crucial it is that tech companies play their part in combating child sexual abuse'.

'It is vital that Facebook do not press ahead without amending their current end-to-end-encryption plans, otherwise sick criminals like Wilson could still be abusing children with impunity,' the home secretary added.

Chief Constable Simon Bailey, the national policing lead for child protection, said: 'The information from Facebook was crucial in bringing Wilson to justice. Which is why I am concerned about Facebook planning to introduce further encryption and privacy protections, making it harder for us to prevent exploitation and find child sexual abusers like Wilson.'

The NCA said Wilson was one of the most prolific paedophiles they had ever investigated and mainly used Facebook Messenger for his abuse.

Mr Jones believes he would not have been caught if the service had been encrypted while Wilson was targeting victims.

He said the predator was identified through a 'cyber tip' regime that currently sees more than half of referrals come from Facebook.

The NCA estimates that there is a minimum of 300,000 people who present a sexual threat to children in the UK.

Around 4,500 offenders were arrested and 6,000 children safeguarded in 2020, and Mr Jones said an 'awful lot' of investigations stemmed from the cyber tip regime.

'There will be a lot less referrals and a lot less arrests [if Facebook encrypts its services],' he added. 'We know a large number of Facebook users are seeking to identify children to abuse them.'

He voiced additional concerns that more paedophiles could be drawn away from other platforms to Facebook if its services are encrypted, causing a wider fall in referrals to the NCA.

'There is a potential domino effect where offenders will coalesce where they think they are safe,' Mr Jones said.

'We're not asking for anything more than we currently have. This isn't about privacy or security on their networks, we're asking to maintain a position where Facebook can access their own material and report the unlawful abuse of children to the NCA and international law enforcement'

Mr Jones said the NCA had been in discussions with Facebook about its concerns but was unhappy with current assurances.

'I implore them to not create a risk and fail in their duty of care,' he added. 'They must explain how they mitigate the risk from those new measures.'

Facebook said it would still be able to make metadata available to law enforcement and continue sending cyber tips based on user reports, and evidence from profile photos and group descriptions.

'Child exploitation and grooming have no place on our platforms,' a spokesperson said. 'Facebook has led the industry in developing new ways to prevent, detect, and respond to abuse and we will continue to work with law enforcement to combat criminal activity.

'End-to-end encryption is already the leading technology used by many services to keep people safe online and, when we roll it out on our other messaging services, we will build on our strong anti-abuse capabilities at WhatsApp. For example, through a combination of advanced technology and user reports, WhatsApp bans around 250,000 accounts each month suspected of sharing child exploitative imagery.'

10 February 2021

Northampton teenager joins new campaign by NSPCC to prevent child abuse

'I would like to be part of something really special that invokes change'.

By David Summers

A teenager from Northampton has been recruited by the NSPCC to help the charity prevent child abuse.

Thirteen-year-old Cameron is one of 15 joining a new Board for Change, which has been launched to give young people the chance to help shape the work of the NSPCC across the UK.

Cameron said: 'I would like to be part of something really special that invokes change.

'I'm passionate about travelling and developing my independent skills, and I'd like to do this whilst doing something important and working with other young people from different backgrounds and experiences.

'My focus will be on some of the challenges that affect children and young people, including bullying, racial abuse and poverty. I believe it's important to have safe places to go to in the community and I feel very lucky to have the Emergency Service Cadets.'

A spokesperson for the NSPCC said the pandemic had had a huge impact on young people, with the NSPCC's Childline service carrying out more than 61,000 counselling sessions on mental health since the start of the first lockdown in March last year.

'But as we look to the future, the NSPCC believes it is vital that their voices are represented. The charity is calling for the Government to put young people at the centre of its recovery plans – and as part of this, their views and experiences of the last year must be listened to,' the spokesperson added.

Board members will take part in new experiences and opportunities, meet other young people, as well as develop confidence and learn life-long new skills, such as campaigning and public speaking.

Over a two-year period, members will be involved in sharing what's important to them, take part in residentials, meetings and workshops, and campaign to share their views and opinions.

They met virtually for the first time yesterday, Tuesday.

Lucy Read, NSPCC Associate Head of Participation, said: 'The last year has changed the lives of many young people across the UK but, as we now look to the future, the new members of our Young People's Board for Change have a great opportunity to make their voices heard.

'We received over 300 applications from young people to join the board and during recruitment, I was impressed by the genuine passion young people had for the NSPCC's work and a commitment to get involved and make a difference.

'We believe that a generation of young people should not be defined by the pandemic, so it has never been more important to listen to them and embed their views into everything we do. Children are the experts on their own lives, and there is so much that we can learn from their experiences.'

31 March 2021

Game-changing IWF chatbot to target people trying to access child sexual abuse online

The aim is for the new chatbot to target users before they actually commit a criminal offence.

A game-changing new interactive chatbot will interrupt people trying to access online child sexual abuse material to get them to change their ways.

The End Violence Fund has recently announced the funding grant for the new Internet Watch Foundation (IWF) reThink chatbot which the charity has been developing.

The IWF is the UK charity responsible for finding and removing images and videos of children suffering sexual abuse from the internet. They are also part of the UK Safer Internet Centre, working with Childnet International and the SWGfL to promote the safe and responsible use of technology for children and young people.

The new reThink Chatbot will engage with internet users who are showing signs that they might be looking for images of child sexual abuse.

It will attempt to engage users in a friendly and supportive conversation and at the right time, signpost and refer them to the IWF's partner organisation, The Lucy Faithfull Foundation, which could help them change and control their behaviour.

The aim is for the chatbot to target these users at that moment, before they actually commit a criminal offence.

The IWF can engage with them, alert them to behaviour that is illegal online and inform them that help is available for them to control their inappropriate sexual behaviour.

The chatbot is planned to be fully working and rolled out by the end of 2022.

The Lucy Faithfull Foundation runs the Stop It Now! UK & Ireland helpline as well as deterrence campaigns and intervention programs to prevent child sexual abuse, including the Stop It Now! Get Help website which provides self-help for people viewing child sexual abuse material and receives 15,000 visitors a month.

In March, the National Crime Agency (NCA) revealed it believes there are a minimum of 300,000 individuals in the UK posing a sexual threat to children, either through physical 'contact' abuse or online.

In 2019, the Internet Watch Foundation had a record year, with analysts processing 260,400, up from 229,328 reports in 2018. Of these reports, 132,700 showed images and/or videos of children being sexually abused. This compares to 105,047 reports of child sexual abuse material in 2018

This has been accelerated during the coronavirus crisis. Data published in July showed the IWF received 44,809 reports from members of the public between March 23 and July 9 this year.

Please remember, images and videos of online child sexual abuse can be reported anonymously at https://report.iwf.org.uk/en

The public is given this advice when making a report:

♦ Do report images and videos of child sexual abuse to the IWF to be removed. Reports to the IWF are anonymous.

♦ Do provide the exact URL where child sexual abuse images are located.

♦ Don't report other harmful content – you can find details of other agencies to report to on the IWF's website.

♦ Do report to the police if you are concerned about a child's welfare.

♦ Do report only once for each web address – or URL. Repeat reporting of the same URL isn't needed and wastes analysts' time.

♦ Do report non-photographic visual depictions of the sexual abuse of children, such as computer-generated images. Anything of this nature, which is also hosted in the UK, the IWF can get removed.

22 October 2020

Where can I find help?

Below are some telephone numbers, email addresses and websites of agencies or charities that can offer support or advice if you, or someone you know needs it.

If you think someone is in immediate danger call the police on 999 or the NSPCC on 0808 800 5000 without delay.

Childline
0800 1111 (24 hours)
www.childline.org.uk

NSPCC
0808 800 5000 (24 hours, every day)
www.nspcc.org.uk

Child Exploitation and Online Protection Command
www.ceop.police.uk/ceop-reporting/

The Mix
0808 808 4994
www.themix.org.uk

NAPAC (National Association of People Abused in Childhood)
0808 801 0331
www.napac.org.uk

The Maggie Oliver Foundation
help@themaggieoliverfoundation.com
www.themaggieoliverfoundation.com

Safeline
Women 0808 802 9999
Men   0808 800 5005
Young People 0808 800 5007
Text 07860 027 573
www.safeline.org.uk

The Survivors Trust
Support, Advice & Info: 0808 801 0818
www.thesurvivorstrust.org

RASASC (Rape and Sexual Abuse Support Centre)
National Helpline 0808 802 9999 (12-2.30 & 7-9.30)
www.rasasc.org.uk

Rape Crisis
www.rapecrisis.org.uk

Family Matters - Rape and sexual abuse support services
Helpline 01474 537392
www.familymattersuk.org
Women Against Rape
www.womenagainstrape.net

Survivors UK – Male Rape & Sexual Abuse
www.survivorsuk.org

Stop it Now! UK & Ireland - helping prevent child sexual abuse
Confidential Helpline - 0808 1000 900
www.stopitnow.org.uk

Internet Watch Foundation
www.iwf.org.uk

Freedom Charity - for help and advice on forced marriage, honour based violence and FGM
0845 607 0133
Text 4freedom to 88802
www.freedomcharity.org.uk

Karma Nirvana - supporting victims of honour-based abuse and forced marriage.
0800 5999 247
www.karmanirvana.org.uk

Samaritans
116 123
www.samaritans.org

Victim Support
08 08 16 89 111
www.victimsupport.org.uk

Key Facts

- One in five adults aged 18 to 74 years experienced at least one form of child abuse, whether emotional abuse, physical abuse, sexual abuse, or witnessing domestic violence or abuse, before the age of 16 years. (page 2)

- 1 in 100 adults aged 18 to 74 years experienced physical neglect before the age of 16 years. (page 2)

- 3.1 million adults aged 18 to 74 years were victims of sexual abuse before the age of 16 years. (page 2)

- Around one in four women (25%; 5.1 million) and around one in six men (16%; 3.3 million) experienced abuse before the age of 16 years. (page 3)

- Around half of adults (52%) who experienced abuse before the age of 16 years also experienced domestic abuse later in life. (page 3)

- Half of all children on child protection plans in England are on plans because of concerns about neglect. (page 12)

- 1 in 10 children will have experienced neglect – i.e. potentially 3 children in every class of 30. (page 12)

- 137,000 Women and girls are living with the consequences of FGM in the UK. (page 14)

- Forced marriages were criminalised in 2014. (page 18)

- Between 2006 and 2016, 3,354 marriages involving children aged 16 to 17 were registered in England and Wales. (page 18)

- One-in-five UK adults (20%) think that its less concerning for a woman to be abusing a teenage boy than a man to be abusing a teenage girl and, of these, nearly two-thirds (64%) said it was because they think teenage girls are more vulnerable than teenage boys. More than a quarter (28%) thought it was every teenage boy's dream to be with an older woman. (page 20)

- More than a quarter of child sexual abuse victims are boys. (page 21)

- 15% of girls and 5% of boys experience some form of sexual abuse before the age of 16. (page 21)

- 17% of men thought that a woman in her 30s and a 16-year-old boy exchanging text messages containing explicit images was not concerning, compared to 2% of women. (page 21)

- The UK's child abuse image database has 17 million unique images on it, and it is growing by 500,000 every two months. (page 23)

- Between April and September 2020, 4,700 people, nearly all men, were arrested for online child abuse offences and more than 6,000 children were safeguarded. (page 24)

- 7.5% of adults aged 18 to 74 years experienced sexual abuse before they were 16. (page 26)

- 18,700 children had been identified as suspected victims of child sexual exploitation in 2018/19. (page 26)

- Abused or neglected children are four times more likely to develop serious mental illness. (page 29)

- 81% of child sexual abuse survivors feel stereotyped. (page 30)

- The UK received 12 million tips over child sex abuse images and suspicious activity from Facebook in 2020. (page 36)

- In 2019, the Internet Watch Foundation had a record year, with analysts processing 260,400, up from 229,328 reports in 2018. Of these reports, 132,700 showed images and/or videos of children being sexually abused. This compares to 105,047 reports of child sexual abuse material in 2018. (page 38)

Glossary

Bullying

A form of aggressive behaviour used to intimidate someone. It can be inflicted both physically and mentally (psychologically).

Child abuse

The emotional, physical or sexual mistreatment of a child (person under the age of 18). Also includes neglect.

Child exploitation

Child exploitation is a broad term which includes forced or dangerous labour, child trafficking and child prostitution. The term is used to refer to situations where children are abused - physically, verbally or sexually - or when they are submitted to unsatisfactory conditions as part of their forced or voluntary employment.

Child marriage

Where children, often before they have reached puberty, are given to be married – often to a person many years older.

Child Protection Plan

A plan detailing what must be done to promote a child`s development and health along with protecting them from further harm.

Child sexual exploitation (CSE)

Using or exploiting a child for sexual purposes. This often goes hand-in-hand with the grooming process and can involve offering the child money, gifts, cigarettes or alcohol in return for sexual favours. CSE can lead to child trafficking and prostitution.

Crime

Crime may be defined as an act or omission prohibited or punished by law. A 'criminal offence' includes any infringement of the criminal law, from homicide to riding a bicycle without lights. What is classified as a crime is supposed to reflect the values of society and to reinforce those values. If an act is regarded as harmful to society or its citizens, it is often, but not always, classified as a criminal offence.

Cyberbullying

Cyberbullying is when technology is used to harass, embarrass or threaten to hurt someone. A lot is done through social networking sites such as Facebook and Twitter. Bullying via mobile phones is also a form of cyberbullying. With the use of technology on the rise, there are more and more incidents of cyberbullying.

Digital abuse

Most frequently occurring in teenage relationships, digital abuse involves the use of texting and social networking sites to keep track of, harass, stalk, control, bully or intimidate a partner.

Emotional abuse

Emotional abuse refers to a victim being verbally attacked, criticised and put down. Following frequent exposure to this abuse, the victim's mental wellbeing suffers as their self-esteem is destroyed and the perpetrator's control over them increases. They may suffer from feelings of worthlessness, believing that they deserve the abuse or that if they were to leave the abuser they would never find another partner.

A victim may also have been convinced by their abuser that the abuse is their fault. The abuser can use these feelings to manipulate the victim.

Exploitation

Taking advantage of or using someone for selfish reasons.

Female genital mutilation (FGM)

FGM is a non-medical cultural practice that involves partially or totally removing a girl or woman's external genitalia.

Grooming

Actions that are deliberately performed in order to encourage a child to engage in sexual activity. For example, offering friendship and establishing an emotional connection, buying gifts, etc.

In need

If the quality of a child`s health or development is likely to be impaired unless provided by a local authority.

Internet Watch Foundation

A charity that works to minimise the availability of child abuse images and other criminal adult content on the Internet.

Mandatory reporting

The reporting of a crime or criminal behaviour that is required by law.

Neglect (emotional and physical)

A failure to sufficiently care for the needs of something or someone.

Physical abuse

Physical abuse involves the use of violence or force against a victim and can including hitting, slapping, kicking, pushing, strangling or other forms of violence. Physical assault is a crime and the police have the power to protect victims, but in a domestic violence situation it can sometimes take a long time for the violence to come to light. Some victims are too afraid to go to the police, believe they can reform the abuser (who they may still love), or have normalised their abusive situation and do not realise they can get help.

Rape

Forcing someone to engage in sexual intercourse against their will. Force is not necessarily physical, it could also be emotional or psychological.

Sarah's Law

Campaigned for after the murder of Sarah Payne, the scheme allows parents to enquire about a named individual to establish whether they are a known sex-offender. Also called the Child Sex Offender Disclosure Scheme.

Sexual abuse

Sexual abuse occurs when a victim is forced into a sexual act against their will, through violence or intimidation. This can include rape. Sexual abuse is always a crime, no matter what the relationship is between the victim and perpetrator.

Activities

Brainstorming

♦ What are some of the organisations who help victims of child abuse? Make a list of the ones that you know.

♦ Make a list of people who can you speak to if you need support.

♦ In small groups, make a positive/negative list of family behaviours (do not use personal experiences).

♦ Create a diamond 9 of ways to get help and support. Put the most useful at the top and least useful at the bottom.

♦ Make a list of the reasons children may stay quiet about abuse they have experienced.

Research

♦ In pairs, research child marriage. In which countries is it legal? What is the youngest age of marriage? Do any of your findings surprise you?

♦ Research which countries have a ban on smacking children. Present your findings in an infograph.

♦ Research how abuse can be reported and who it can be reported to.

Design

♦ Design a poster for a safe learning environment - include some class rules.

♦ Design a leaflet drawing attention to the issue of FGM. Include some statistics.

♦ Choose an article from this topic and design an illustration that highlights its key message.

♦ Create a leaflet that will be distributed to parents of children aged 11–13 advising how they can help keep their children safe online.

♦ Design a leaflet to inform people on what grooming is and how to recognise the signs of being groomed.

Oral

♦ In small groups, discuss who can be a trusted adult. Do you know how to access the pastoral team or safeguarding lead at your school? How might someone approach them to start a difficult conversation?

♦ In pairs, discuss the issue of 'neglect'. Write down some examples of neglectful behaviour and then consider the effects that each behaviour might have on a child. For example, failing to keep a child clean and clothed is considered neglectful behaviour and could affect that child's health and experiences at school.

♦ 'Failure to report child abuse should become a criminal offence'. Debate this statement as a class, with half of you arguing in favour and half arguing against.

♦ Choose one of the illustrations from this topic and, in pairs, discuss why you think the artist chose to portray the issue the way they did.

Reading/Writing

♦ Imagine you have a friend called Ali who has been having a difficult time at home and needs help. Write an answer for each of the following:

· What might Ali say?

· Who can Ali speak to for help?

· Why might someone need help?

· Where might someone find reliable sources of help?

· When would be the best time to speak to someone?

♦ Using the information from this book, write a short paragraph summarising the definition of 'child abuse'.

♦ Choose an article from this book and write a one paragraph summary. Then list three key points from the article.

♦ Write an article on the use of social media and how it can increase the risk of child abuse.

♦ Imagine you work for a charity which campaigns against child marriage in the UK. Write a blog-post for your charity's website explaining the issues surrounding child marriage and your feelings about the issue.

♦ Write an article for your school/college newspaper explaining why it is important to seek help if you have been abused. Include some information about charities and centres that can help.

Acknowledgements

The publisher is grateful for permission to reproduce the material in this book. While every care has been taken to trace and acknowledge copyright, the publisher tenders its apology for any accidental infringement or where copyright has proved untraceable. The publisher would be pleased to come to a suitable arrangement in any such case with the rightful owner.

The material reproduced in *ISSUES* books is provided as an educational resource only. The views, opinions and information contained within reprinted material in *ISSUES* books do not necessarily represent those of Independence Educational Publishers and its employees.

Images

Cover image courtesy of iStock. All other images courtesy of Freepik, Pixabay and Unsplash,

Illustrations

Simon Kneebone: pages 8 & 31. Angelo Madrid: pages 5, 17 & 33.

Additional acknowledgements

With thanks to the Independence team: Shelley Baldry, Danielle Lobban, Jackie Staines and Jan Sunderland.

Tracy Biram

Cambridge, May 2021